Up Your Aspirations

Negotiating program using NLP

Robert Smith

Pau Publications

Published in the United Kingdom by:

Pau Publications

The Caldecott Centre
163 Clifton Road, Rugby
Warwickshire CV21 3QN

A catalogue record for this book
is available from the British Library

Typeset in the United Kingdom by:
Pau Publications, 163 Clifton Road, Rugby
Warwickshire CV21 3QN

Printed and bound in the United Kingdom

A ohe pau ko ike i kou halau

'Think not that all wisdom is in your school'

Ancient Hawai'ian saying

Acknowledgements

Any book is the product of many people. I would like to acknowledge the help and assistance of past course participants and colleagues, who jointly motivated me to turn my negotiating training courses into this book.

Colleagues who have helped and supported me during the writing of the book include Lesley MacKay, Graham Whiting, Dave Marshall and Ron Bowles. Other colleagues who have contributed include Phil Williams, Pam Weight, Ralph Watson, Caroline Suggett, Wyatt Woodsmall and Ian Monde.

I am grateful to the inspiration of my American associate partner Keith Clarke. Thanks to Roger Day, my friend and training associate in excellent writing and editing skills, for making writing such fun.

Finally, I appreciate the never ending help and support of my wife, Lynn, and the uncomplaining attitude of my dog, King. Long may we negotiate life together!

Robert Smith
March 1996

Foreword to second edition

So, here we are again at the beginning of a new millenium with the second edition **Up Your Aspirations.** The success of the book owes a great deal to the continuing support of a number of major organisations who use it as the standard text for their negotiating, influencing and persuading training.

I personally have had the pleasure of working with, among others, National Air Traffic Services, Anglia Water/CSC, Motorola UK, IBM, Air Miles, Vardon, A C Neilsen, Powergen, Blackwell, Outward Bound, Cable & Wireless, British Aerospace, Public Health Laboratories Services, Tesco, Boots, London Electricity, Hong Kong & Shanghai Bank, Aspect Telecommunications and British Telecommunications.

Since the first edition I have extended my skillbase by becoming a Master Trainer of Neuro-Linguistic Programming. Along with these new skills I have been able to develop more leadership and personal development programmes which have been of specific benefit for those who work in information technology, engineering and the scientific fields. My experience is that people who have a high IQ (intelligence quotient) frequently have a low EQ (emotional quotient). Success depends on the skills of EQ rather than merely having a high IQ.

My aim at the start of this millenium is to negotiate with organisations to provide the tools needed to maximise people's EQ.

Robert Smith
January 2000

Contents

Negotiation: Confer (with another) with a view to compromise or agreement

Oxford English Dictionary

Introduction

Introduction

Have you ever suffered buyer's remorse? At first you experience the euphoria and thrill of buying something—a new car, the house of your dreams, a state-of-the-art home computer system.

Time passes, and the euphoria you first knew turns to bitter disappointment. Now you realise with Shakespeare that all that glisters truly is not gold. Even the gold leaf has peeled away. You regret you ever went ahead with the deal. And you feel somehow you've been cheated.

That's buyer's remorse.

This book will ensure that buyer's remorse never happens to you again. By following the practical steps in this book you'll become an *excellent negotiator* in your personal and business dealings. You'll learn how to make sure that all parties leave the negotiation feeling they've won. As an excellent negotiator you'll genuinely want everyone to get something good out of the deal.

I call this a *win-win* outcome.

There are several other possible outcomes to negotiation. Both parties end up losing *(lose-lose)*, one party gains to the detriment of the other *(win-lose* or *lose-win)* or the negotiation doesn't reach a conclusion *(no outcome)*. The most successful negotiator aims for a win-win outcome so that all parties feel positive about the deal and are willing to negotiate again. There's no room for buyer's remorse in a win-win outcome.

Everyone wants a bargain. That's human nature. Using the techniques outlined in this book you'll end up getting a bargain and ensuring the other person gets one, too. Instead of 'pulling a fast one' you'll learn to co-operate with the other person.

The danger of a book of this sort is that you might be tempted to go out and misuse the information. Unscrupulous negotiators could master the skills in this book and then use them to win every deal at the expense of the other person. They could easily use this material to manipulate people.

Doing this carries a *health warning:* Once bitten, the other person will never want to do business with you again. After all, would you go back to buy more apples from a market stall when you were cheated with a bag of mouldy, misshapen or under-ripe apples the first time round?

As an excellent negotiator, your aim is to build a long-term relationship with people. To do this you need to move away from game-playing tactics towards an open, honest relationship in which you can achieve your objectives.

Let me give you an example. A man I know wanted to sort out a pension plan and couldn't at the time afford the monthly

NEGOTIATING NUGGET:

Always work for a win-win outcome for all parties concerned, unless you never want the other side to talk to you again.

payments needed.

His financial adviser had an idea. 'I can help you set up a pension scheme that effectively won't cost you anything for two years,' he said. 'My idea is that I help you to transfer your mortgage from one building society to another.'

Because of the pressure on financial institutions at the time, building societies were offering a two per cent reduction in mortgage repayments for the first two years of a new mortgage. This would release about £70 a month to buy a pension. At the end of the two-year period, hopefully this man's financial situation would be more settled.

'What happens if you arrange the transfer for me and I decide not to have the pension?' he asked.

'That would be my loss—and I'm still willing to help you,' the financial adviser said.

As a result, the man moved his mortgage to another building society and took out a pension plan. He was happy because he had started his pension, his financial adviser was happy because he had gained some business and the new building society was happy because they had an extra customer. It was a win-win situation for all parties, especially as the man with the mortgage received the cost of the solicitor's fees from the building society to make the transfer.

This book will show you step by step how to become an excellent negotiator. Each chapter has a summary at the end to remind you of the most important points. The book is divided into sections to coincide with the three aspects of negotiation: talking the same language, planning and the process. However, it's important to realise that these three aspects of negotiation are interrelated.

The negotiating program outlined in this book is based on Neuro Linguistic Programming (NLP). In this we study the psychology of excellence. *Neuro* relates to the brain and how we filter through the senses our experience of the world. *Linguistic* refers to the words and body language we use to communicate. *Programming* is the thinking strategies we use consistently to get the outcome we want.

None of us can replicate a person's brain; we can, however, model the excellent negotiator's linguistics and the thinking and behavioural programs. That is precisely what this book does.

How can an average negotiator become an excellent negotiator? Reading a book is only one aspect. In order for the principles to become a part of you it's important to hear how they work, see them in action and practise them.

The way to practise them is all day, every day. Whatever you are doing, selling or buying, negotiate until you've developed your own negotiating program. Then it becomes a reflex action. Finally, you relish the notion of entering the lion's den of business negotiation.

Once you've learned the principles and mastered the techniques of an excellent negotiator you'll be able to go out and get a better deal for all parties concerned.

Robert Smith
May 1996

Part One: Talking the Same Language

1
How to Succeed Every Time

Excellent negotiators have learned the art of succeeding in every negotiation they are involved in. How? By developing skills in a wide range of areas.

For instance, excellent negotiators combine understanding of human nature with sound business judgment. They must be logical analysers and at the same time good with people. The person who is financially driven isn't always good with people, and the person who is good with people doesn't always take naturally to numbers. The excellent negotiator must have a balance of the two.

Negotiation is never one person negotiating with another. It is two organisations facing each other across the negotiating table, even if this is represented only by one person on each side. We all work as part of a team. Even the sole trader may need advice from the bank manager and/or an accountant.

What happens if at the moment you are good with people and not at numbers? For you it is particularly important to work as part of a *negotiating team* so that the other team members balance their strengths with your areas for development. (I use the phrase 'areas for development' in place of 'weaknesses'. I see every individual as potentially able to develop these areas for themselves or will 'know a man who can'.)

For you, being part of a team rather than working on your own provides a far better way of working towards a win-win outcome for all parties concerned.

Becoming a team player is just one aspect. I offer the following list of 15 ideas as a reference point for you to think in terms of your personal strengths and areas for development:

1. Become a team player

Sometimes it isn't worth spending vast amounts of time and effort strengthening your areas for development when you can get someone else to do that part of the work instead! Being part of a team frees you up to work in the areas you're really good at. As an excellent negotiator you can learn to use the people you have available in your organisation to build an effective negotiating team that is working towards a win-win outcome for all concerned.

NEGOTIATING NUGGET:

Excellent negotiators learn how to be team players rather than loners.

2. Cultivate support

In the same way as you negotiate with customers, learn to negotiate with people in your own organisation—the boss, the accounts department, the distribution section and your own negotiating team. It's vitally important for you as an excellent negotiator to win the confidence and support of your own team and organisation.

3. Plan to plan

Excellent negotiators spend more time planning than average negotiators do (see chapter 6: 'Seven Steps to Planning Negotiations'). They plan the overall process and also develop a detailed knowledge of the goods and services being sold or bought. Excellent negotiators are diligent at doing their homework. They get to know the products or services and what benefits they are to the customer. Such negotiators check out the facts they already have and probe for yet more information.

4. Develop sound business judgment

Ask the question: 'What are the real bottom-line issues in this deal?' It's no good selling a million cases of tinned baked beans if every time you do so you lose £3 a case. Think: 'How does the deal we're striking affect the organisation and eventually the bottom line?' You may be packaging and bargaining a number of products, or the negotiation may be on a pan-European or pan-global basis. When it comes down to it, however, what are the business issues and how well do you understand them? Negotiation is more than two people talking to each other; it's about two businesses negotiating and how that affects them now and in the future.

5. Grow in handling ambiguity and conflict

Conflict will turn up in many negotiations. The other person may use aggressive tactics (see chapter 9: 'Black Belt Techniques'). People can be ambiguous and unclear. The excellent negotiator learns how to take these companions in his or her stride and rechannel the energy, using it to aim for a win-win outcome for everyone concerned.

6. Set higher targets

There's a vast amount of research proving that people who set higher targets get better results. The best negotiators have high aspirations and achieve a win-win situation for everyone (see chapter 14: 'Up Your Aspirations'). You may be shooting for the stars and only get to the moon, but at least that's better than only getting to Clapham Junction! The excellent negotiator has the courage to set higher targets and learns to take the risks that go with those targets.

7. Learn to listen

Excellent negotiators have the common sense to listen with an open mind. They are constantly speculating and assuming things but they always thoroughly check their speculations and assumptions before acting. They are patient, listening to and waiting for the whole story to unfold. They ask lots of good questions and they draw out the story the other person has to tell (see chapter 5: 'Listening and Questioning Skills'). Until you know that story, how do you know where to go next in your discussions?

8. Get involved

The excellent negotiator gets involved with the other person's organisation. It's often important to talk to people within that organisation, including the boss, the accounts department and the production staff. Start developing personal as well as business relationships with them (see chapter 4: 'Building Rapport'). The more you know about the organisation the better you'll be able to come up with new ways to negotiate which will be better for all sides.

NEGOTIATING NUGGET:

Make sure you are consistent in what you say and how you say it. Otherwise the other party will notice the leakage.

9. Seek mutual satisfaction

Look for ways for the other side to continue to want to work with you. Be committed to integrity. Once you've negotiated with them, continue looking for ways to increase their satisfaction. 'Do to others what you would have them do to you.'

10. Have an enquiring mind

Excellent negotiators have a genuinely open mind. They're curious to know what's going on. They're fascinated by people and the way they interact with others. They constantly probe for yet more information. Asking questions is a way of entering the other person's frame of reference and thus building rapport.

11. Come to understand people

As an excellent negotiator you'll want to know how people tick. You'll seek to understand their individual personalities. You'll start finding out about and showing an interest in their family, hobbies and leisure pursuits. All these personal issues can affect the outcome of the negotiation.

12. Become confident

Because excellent negotiators have done their planning and have learnt their subject, they come into all negotiations with a high measure of self-confidence. If you are self-confident and have rapport with people it makes the relationship far stronger. When you meet people who have self-confidence it's infectious. They are people who ooze confidence, not arrogance. They seem to say: 'I know what I'm talking about. I've done my homework. I know where I'm going. Now let's do business.'

Self-confidence is based on the person having done the planning, obtained the information and learned how to negotiate. Arrogance takes a different route: 'I don't need to do the planning. I don't need the information. And I certainly don't need to go on a negotiating course!'

NEGOTIATING NUGGET:

Build rapport with the other party. Make sure you contact before you contract.

13. Be willing to bring in experts

Excellent negotiators don't know everything about everything. They will bring in specialists who can help in the process of negotiation. These might include technical or accountancy experts or those whose position and influence may be needed to bring the negotiation to a quick conclusion (see chapter 13: 'The Power Balance').

14. Have a sense of humour

There are a lot of ambiguities, conflicts, deadlines, deadlocks and pressures in negotiation. It's important, therefore, that excellent negotiators have a lively sense of humour—and good timing of that humour. They can learn to keep smiling through it all. I believe that one of the first signs of stress is that people lose their sense of humour.

Humour includes more than just telling jokes. It involves learning how to ride the sea of stress with a smile on your face. After all, negotiation is a very stressful business to be in. It's tempting to become touchy and abrasive when you're under pressure. Instead, keep your sense of humour and you'll be able to succeed.

15. Be happy with yourself

Excellent negotiators know they're OK in themselves. They have done their own personal negotiation and have the stability no longer to take things personally. While they demand respect, they aren't constantly looking for people to like, recognise or praise them. People who aren't OK with themselves can become vulnerable, especially under the pressure of negotiation. As an excellent negotiator you will like yourself and speak positively about your attributes. And you won't always be looking to others to like you.

Summary

Consider again the 15 keys to becoming a successful negotiator:

1. **Become a team player**
2. **Cultivate support**
3. **Plan to plan**
4. **Develop sound business judgment**
5. **Grow in handling ambiguity and conflict**
6. **Set higher targets**
7. **Learn to listen**
8. **Get involved**
9. **Seek mutual satisfaction**
10. **Have an enquiring mind**
11. **Come to understand people**
12. **Become confident**
13. **Be willing to bring in experts**
14. **Have a sense of humour**
15. **Be happy with yourself**

Before you continue reading this book, stop and consider each of these keys to success. What do you need to do in order to develop each one of them? If you identify a deficiency, think about it as an area for development, not a sign of weakness. It doesn't necessarily mean you can't negotiate.

Once you've identified areas for development, consider ways to plug the gaps. You may want to find someone with a strength in that area to work alongside you on the negotiating team until you feel confident enough to go it alone.

2
The Helping Handful

Successful negotiation is about *each side feeling good about the deal.* If both parties win, there is no bitter aftertaste or feeling that we've somehow been cheated or let down. Repeat business is therefore almost guaranteed. Always remember that *negotiation is about long-term relationships, not short-term triumphs.* (Mind you, such triumphs are nice to have!)

Recently I offered a training course to a major US company. The course happened to be about negotiation—and, as with any other course, I needed to negotiate the arrangements with the company. I told the company I believed the course could save them money. They offered me the chance to put this to the test. We were both in a win-win situation about this initial negotiation.

On the very first day of the course one of the participants followed a negotiating technique I'd taught. During the lunch break he made a phone call and negotiated a successful deal. This one course alone proved that it would pay for everyone else in the company to come on it. Even better, the overall gains to the company's bottom line are still being counted every day, long after the courses have finished.

NEGOTIATING NUGGET:

Build good relationships with the other side and your negotiations will always be successful.

Helping hand

What, then, makes a successful negotiation? I believe that first and foremost the negotiator needs to be aware of the five elements in every negotiation.

Think of a hand. A hand needs five digits—four fingers and a thumb—to function fully. If one is missing, the hand isn't working as well as it could have done. In the same way, there are five elements (or digits) in any successful negotiation. Leave out one and the negotiation will be incomplete. The five elements are:
☐ **Competition**
☐ **Co-operation**
☐ **Organisation**
☐ **Attitude**
☐ **Personal factors**

1. Competition

Competition is one of the most obvious elements of negotiation. It's often the first thing people think about when the word 'negotiation' is mentioned. If it is missing or considered insignificant, the deal is unlikely to result in a win-win situation.

I was working in the southern USA a while back and on the last day crossed the border into Mexico for lunch. While there I decided to buy my wife a beautifully decorated piece of pottery. The pottery was on sale at 'Only $15 each'. Here was a situation where I knew I could use my negotiating skills.

After watching for a time I worked out that tourists were paying $11 or $12 after a bit of haggling. So I went up to the salesman and began negotiating with an opening offer.

'I'll give you $7 for one of those.'

'Yes,' he said.

Immediately I felt deflated. How dare he accept my first price! The wind had gone out of my negotiating sails and I'd lost the deal. Instead of thinking, 'At least I did better than the other tourists,' I thought, 'If I'd tried I could have got a better deal.'

Looking back I would have been far happier to have negotiated with him and paid $10. At least I would have haggled over the price. As it was, *I* wasn't happy because I could have got it for less. I had broken my own golden rule: *'Aim higher and do better, or up your aspiration.'*

Aim higher and do better, or up your aspiration

The converse is equally true. Many people engaged in negotiation immediately leap to number crunching. They have a fixation on the cost and nothing else matters. They think of negotiation as the kind of bartering that goes on in a Middle Eastern market. You offer to sell for £50,000 and I offer to buy for £30,000. Eventually we meet somewhere in the middle.

That has a limiting effect because it doesn't get everyone the best possible result. Of course, a good negotiator has to deal with this part of the negotiation. But it mustn't be at the expense of others. Good negotiation is highly ethical. It never involves knocking the competition. When I negotiate I either talk about my competitors in glowing terms or I say nothing about them at all.

There are several tactics in the competition stakes that can be used to get a better outcome for yourself. On their own, though, they result in a win-lose situation—I win at the expense of the other person. I want to focus on a good outcome for all parties, not just myself. I want a win-win outcome. Nevertheless, you need to know the tactics and the counter-measures because you never know who you might come up against!

2. Co-operation

The second element of negotiation, co-operation, involves finding the common ground between the two parties. How can we discover a way for both parties to get a better outcome? Once that way is found, people will be more willing to compromise to achieve their goals.

NEGOTIATING NUGGET:

The most successful negotiator wants both sides to succeed.

Co-operation, involves finding the common ground between the two parties

Co-operation was the basis of the 1974 Camp David agreement between the two former enemy states Israel and Egypt. Negotiators found the common ground between the two countries and a deal was struck. That agreement still stands today.

Suppose you and I decide to buy a car between us. We disagree on what car we want. You want a Ford and I want a Vauxhall. But we *do* agree on the fact that we both want a car.

In the process of negotiation it's possible to lose sight of such obvious wants both parties have in common. Then you can find ways of packaging and bargaining things so that both parties can get a better deal.

In our case we are agreed that we both want a car. There are also things you want in a car and things I want in a car. We can leave aside the Ford and Vauxhall labels and work out the common areas: We both want an engine of at least 1.8 litres, metallic blue finish, ABS brakes, airbags, fuel injection. Once we've found the things we both want, we can list all the makes of car that meet our criteria. We will then be focusing on *agreement* rather than *disagreement*.

This focusing on agreement can be applied to two individuals, two companies or even two nations.

There's a real art to finding that common ground and building on it. It's still necessary to overcome the conflict, but what a much better place to start a negotiation from—a point of agreement!

There are whole patterns of the way we use language and the way we come to agreement that can be learned (see chapter 3: 'What Makes People Tick?').

I was running an advanced training course in negotiation and another course in presentation for a major company recently. There were five days of training in all. I didn't want to lower my price and they wanted a good deal for a fairly large investment. By putting the training package into one whole week we were able to go to a hotel in co-operation with each other and book the accommodation and conference facilities at a much more favourable rate. The overall cost to my customer was a lot less and I was able to keep my fees at the normal level.

I was happy because I was able to charge my normal fee. The company was happy because it saved on accommodation. And the hotelier was happy because we filled an otherwise potentially empty hotel. It was win-win-win!

3. Organisation

Of the five elements of negotiation, organisation is perhaps the most important. If you and I are negotiating about something, you'll be negotiating for someone else in your organisation and I'll be negotiating for someone in mine. Sometimes it's easy to forget this aspect.

There might be only two people sitting around the negotiating table, yet it's really two organisations involved. I need to ask myself: 'In what way can people in my organisation help this person to negotiate with whoever he (or she) is negotiating with?' or: 'What sort of leverage do we as an organisation have that we can put on the purchaser's people?'

There might be only two people sitting around the negotiating table, yet it's really two organisations involved

For instance, I could get my technical production manager to talk with your technical director, who would then be convinced that this is the product for you to buy. This would therefore influence you, the purchaser, who is negotiating with me.

My wife wanted to buy a car. She had test-driven this particular one and had fallen in love with it. She was now bursting to own it. Fortunately for us, the man who was selling the car decided for some reason that I was the person buying it. Rather than negotiate with my wife, who probably would have paid the highest price possible to own it, he started to negotiate with me. I wasn't in love with the car in the way my wife was so I managed to get a better price from him than she would have done.

If he'd bothered to think about our organisation (my wife and me), and how we needed to negotiate within our own organisation, he could have made £1000 extra. I know I would have found it impossible to number crunch when faced with my wife and the car salesman both negotiating against me.

You can now see why I believe the internal negotiation within the organisation is often the most difficult part to sort out. There is a real art in ensuring that the whole team is pulling in the same direction. Going out to talk to the customer is often the easiest part.

NEGOTIATING NUGGET:

Remember, it's never just two individuals negotiating; it's always two organisations.

4. Attitude

The attitude of the parties to the negotiation is another element to consider. Have you ever negotiated with a small child who wants an ice cream? When I was a child and I wanted an ice cream I invariably got it. I had the right attitude to negotiate the deal. I wasn't concerned particularly about the flavour or colour; I just wanted an ice cream, and I wanted it *now.*

In all negotiation there must be an attitude of wanting to strike a deal, of desiring to reach a conclusion.

NEGOTIATING NUGGET:

People with the right attitude to negotiating will find a way forward whatever it takes.

If we go into a negotiation with the right kind of attitude, wanting to find the best solution for both sides, we'll succeed

I'm convinced that each of us naturally has all the negotiating ability we need, yet much of it has been socialised out of us. We've become so sophisticated and polite, we don't admit even to ourselves that we want the ice cream.

If we go into a negotiation with the right kind of attitude, wanting to find the best solution for both sides, we'll succeed. If we understand the different personality types and develop the skill to adapt ourselves to whoever we are talking to, we'll get results.

There is a vast difference between this way of negotiating and that of some high pressure salespeople. A salesman may have the attitude: 'There's another gullible mug coming along,' then strike a deal for short-term gains. The negotiator with the right attitude wants a win-win outcome. He or she is out to find ways of reaching the conclusion so that both parties are happy.

Developing the right attitude to negotiation means also having the flexibility of style within yourself to understand other people's attitude and behaviour. It involves building a long-term relationship and ensuring that everyone is happy in the process.

5. Personal factors

Have you ever negotiated with people on the day they are about to go on holiday and they want the deal out of the way? It doesn't take long and it often works in your favour. The more you know about the personal side of your clients the more that can be an advantage to everyone concerned.

Remembering someone's birthday and sending them a card was a principle outlined 40 years ago in the book *How to Win Friends and Influence People.* Yet it's still relevant today. Just as a cat always lands on its feet, thoughtfulness always falls in favour of the person giving the compliment. 'It is more blessed to give than to receive' works in negotiation as in other areas of life.

The more you as the seller know about the buyer, the more it shifts the balance towards you. It's still a win-win outcome for all concerned. It is just that maybe you get 60 per cent and the other person gets 40 per cent. As long as they are happy with the 40 per cent, that's OK.

The more you as the seller know about the buyer, the more it shifts the balance towards you

NEGOTIATING NUGGET:

As William Shakespeare said, 'He who is well paid is well satisfied.'

You never really know what the other person would have settled for. You only know that you and the other person are both satisfied. How satisfied you'll never know—unless you come on a negotiating course and have the opportunity to look at some case studies and discuss them with people afterwards. Then you'll discover how far people will go to be satisfied.

I remember the director of a major organisation on one of my courses being so desperate to do a deal in one of the case studies that he kept selling boxes, and every time he sold one his company lost £1000! He felt that was the whole thing about negotiation—to do some kind of deal. The reality was that the company was running at a loss simply to keep the negotiations going.

I'm not a great believer in special prices for today only, as in the case of supermarket 'loss leaders'. Whatever you negotiate in a deal this time becomes the precedent for negotiation tomorrow. If you give a lot away this time in the hope that you'll get a better deal later, you'll be disappointed. They'll say, 'You gave us 20 per cent discount last time. We want more now.' You need to have a flexibility of style to meet the other side and occasionally you have to be tough with them.

It's certainly about respecting the other person's model of the world. A good negotiator remembers that the other person will only do things for his or her own reasons. Be flexible in your style and deal with others on the level they want to be dealt with.

By learning negotiation skills people will become skilled at spotting certain characteristics in the other side and this will give them major leverage in how best to negotiate with them. You reach the stage where you can learn to play back to them in the style they use. It's almost a case of the other parties negotiating with themselves!

The result is better deals for everyone.

Summary

Remember the five elements in every negotiation:

1. **Competition**
2. **Co-operation**
3. **Organisation**
4. **Attitude**
5. **Personal factors**

Identify any of these elements that you have tended to overlook in negotiations up to now. Reread the relevant text, making notes about what you can do positively to correct any imbalance. Make sure you take into account all five elements in your future negotiations.

3
What Makes People Tick?

In this chapter we look at how the process of communication works. By understanding this you can change the way you communicate with others so that you ensure you can talk their language. The skill is to be able to adjust the way you put things over so that they understand it. Even if the communication isn't perfect, excellent negotiators notice and make changes to ensure that it does work.

The communication process

How does the process of communication work? This is summarised in Diagram 1.

When something happens outside of us *(external event)*, we take in information through our senses—what we see, hear, feel, smell and taste. We then *filter* that information to create our own *internal representation* of that event. These are the pictures we see and hear in our head.

This internal representation affects our emotional *state*. At the same time it affects our body's *physiology,* including our body language. This all then becomes the driving force for our behaviour.

You find yourself in the lion's den. This time it just happens to be during a negotiation. The lion lets out a roar (external event). You know that lions kill people (filter). You know your life is being threatened (internal representation). This is confirmed by a churned-up feeling in your stomach (state) and your body releases adrenalin (physiology). You then instinctively know how to act (behaviour).

This process of survival when dealing with a lion can be developed into a natural, instinctive behaviour when negotiating.

Noticing what you notice

How come we only notice what we're interested in? Neuroscientists estimate that we take in between 2 million and 2.5 million bits of information each *second.* That's a vast amount of information.

NEGOTIATING NUGGET:

The most successful negotiators are the ones with the most flexible style.

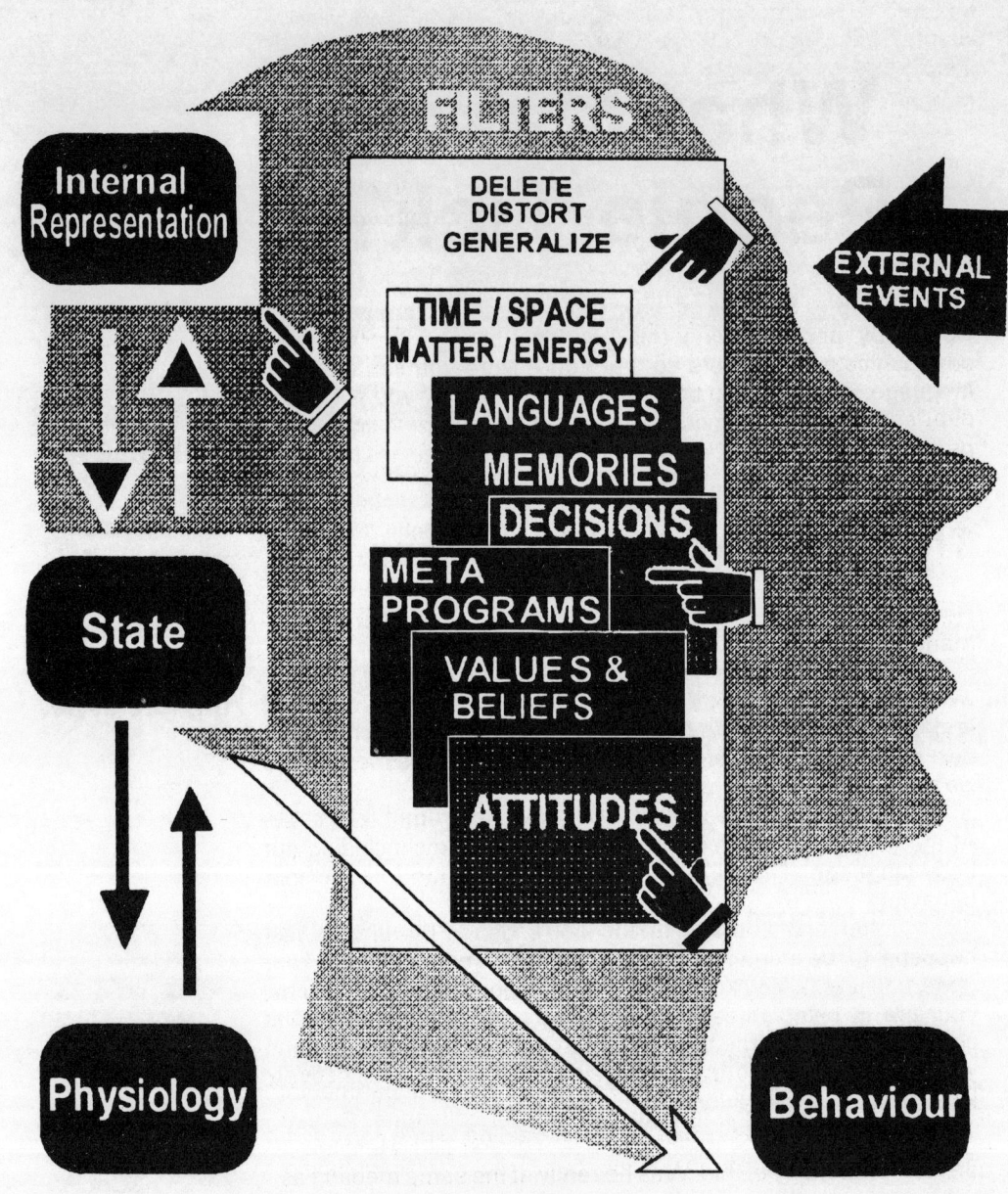

Diagram 1
How we communicate

Right now you're aware of what you're doing with your right foot. At least now that I've mentioned it you are. You weren't aware of this before. You didn't notice the way you were holding this book, but you do now. How come you didn't notice what was going on before? The answer is that you did, but not at a conscious level.

At a conscious level we can only deal with between five and nine pieces of information. Think of as many different models of Ford as you can. If cars are a special interest of yours you might be able to name nine or even ten. If they are of little interest you will be hard pressed to name more than two or three. This is a simple example of noticing what you're interested in.

Another example is when you buy a new car. Suddenly you are amazed how many of that model of car there are on the road. They were there all along, but you didn't notice them before. Your interest is in that car so it has been brought into your awareness.

Recently I've been looking to buy an estate car to take all the equipment I need for training. As I began thinking about this I noticed that every other car on the road seemed to be an estate car!

People can even have a pain while they are working at their computer but not notice it until they move. They have been stiff or in pain all along. It's just that their internal process has been preoccupied.

How filters work

How do we reduce to a manageable level the amount of information coming in? We go through a process of *deleting, distorting* and *generalising* the world through our own built in *filters*. These filters delete, distort and generalise information to reduce it to bite-sized pieces. Let's consider how each of these works.

Delete

When we delete information we simply remove it from our thought process. An example of this is when you've had a departmental meeting. You walk back to your desk with a colleague. As you hear what he has to say about the meeting, you begin to think: 'I don't remember any of this. Was he really at the same meeting as me?'

The truth is that you've both deleted different information from your mind. The five things he remembers have no resemblance to the five things you've remembered. You've remembered the bits you were interested in and haven't even heard the bits he was interested in.

This underlines the importance of agendas, note-taking and minutes in all negotiations.

NEGOTIATING NUGGET:

Find out about the other people's model of the world, and let them know about your model of the world.

Distort

Distortion is where one person perceives an external event differently from another. Two people recently gave an eye witness account of a suspect at a bank robbery. One said he was five feet five inches tall and the other said he was over six feet. One said he was white, the other black. He was the same suspect viewed from two different mental reference points.

I had a motor accident once and agreed with the other person to sort things out with the insurance companies. His version and mine were so different that an outsider would have found it difficult to believe it was the same accident. Neither was wrong; it was just two perspectives of the same event. It must be fun working in an insurance claims office!

Distortion can be useful in negotiation. You can run options through your mind and distort various outcomes. Excellent negotiators use this form of distortion as often as they can because they are always looking for a better deal for everyone.

Generalise

All sentences are generalisations. That includes the one you've just read! Generalisations are often based on life experiences. A woman is frightened of all dogs. She has forgotten the time when she was bitten by a dog when she was a toddler. Now when she sees any dog she experiences terror.

Similarly, someone goes to a soccer match and sees a fight in the terraces. He now holds the belief that all soccer supporters are hooligans. That, of course, is nonsense. If I have a bad experience with a double glazing salesman I might then wrongly assume that all replacement window salespeople are rogues. In each case the person has taken one piece of information and generalised it.

Learning to generalise has its uses. You don't need to put your hand in the fire every time to know it burns. Likewise, if you've been burned by someone you've negotiated with you're not likely to do business with them again. Once bitten, twice shy.

Filters

Having examined the process of communication, we can now examine the way we filter information. If I know what filters are important to you, I can begin to understand you and change my way of communicating with you.

It doesn't matter whether the glass is half full or half empty. If you choose to think of the glass as being half full I will talk with you in those terms. I've understood your filter process and begun to build rapport with you (see chapter 4: 'Building Rapport').

There are many different filters. In this book we will look at just seven:

☐ Language
☐ Memories
☐ Decisions
☐ Perceptions
☐ Values
☐ Beliefs
☐ Attitudes

1. Language

In hundreds of training groups I've run I've asked people to write down words that come to their mind when they think of either 'sex' or 'education'. I allow the groups to decide which one of those two to select and I leave it to your imagination to work out which is the more popular!

There has only ever been one word that everyone in a particular group has included in their list of five words. That group chose 'Education' and all included 'Learning' in their definitions. The fact that only one group had a word in common amazes me. It underlines the power of the language filter and shows me what slippery things words can be.

Most communication is through physiology (body posture, breathing, skin colour, movement) and the use of the voice (tone, timbre, tempo, volume). This leaves only a small percentage for the words. That is why in some organisations there are people who have been very successful and who look and sound like they know what they are talking about. Yet if you listen to their words you realise they're not saying anything. Of course, in your organisation I'm sure you can't identify anyone like this!

It's the old maxim: 'Your actions speak so loud I can't hear what you're saying.'

There are four rules of thumb with the use of language to effect a positive outcome:

a. Say it the way you want it to be

Ask people not to think of a blue tree and what do they think of? Yes, a blue tree! The psychological message of language is far more powerful than the surface message. You cannot not think of a negative!

'I wouldn't want you to think that you might lose this account unless you came up with a better deal. It would be unfair of me to say you might lose this account. It's not down to me to say that you will lose this account. It's down to my boss, which is a separate issue.'

In that short bit of speech I've said three times: 'You will lose this account.' Even though I wasn't saying it, I was getting the

NEGOTIATING NUGGET:

Excellent negotiators label their behaviour: 'Let me make a proposal.' 'I want to summarise what we've done so far.'

message across.

A useful strategy is to load your language to get across the message you want. Tell people what you want to achieve, not what you don't. A good parent will avoid saying to a child: 'Don't drop that tray of glasses' because the tray will almost inevitably fall out of her hands. Instead the parent might say: 'Put that tray of glasses carefully on that table.'

In negotiation you have a choice in how you use language, depending on the effect you want to achieve. In one situation you might want to say: 'I don't want you to think this is hard and is likely to be a very difficult negotiation.' You are inferring here that the negotiation is going to be tough. In another situation you might say: 'This should be simple and is likely to be an easy negotiation.'

On the surface they seem to be the same message yet psychologically they are poles apart.

b. Avoid using weak qualifiers

You've probably met the 'try hopefully' negotiator: 'What I'm going to try to do, hopefully, possibly to explain, with a bit of luck, how to be fairly positive, maybe, about this negotiation.' This kind of person dithers and uses a host of weak qualifiers in every sentence. Would you as a negotiator be convinced such people knew what they were talking about? No way.

The 'try hopefully' negotiator sends a hidden message to the other person: 'I'm not sure what I'm talking about, I think. And I'm likely to be a pushover.' This invites the other party to ask for another concession.

Removing weak qualifiers projects a confident image. Add them and you project an image of uncertainty.

c. Change the buts to ands

I'm enthusiastic about negotiation and people tell me that my enthusiasm is contagious. Then you come along and say: 'Yes, Robert, but . . .' How am I going to react? Immediately it's going to create barriers between us.

If you are looking for win-win for everyone you need to keep open the channels of communication. Instead of introducing a negative, you could say: 'Yes, Robert, *and* . . .' The difference between this and the 'but' reply is that I perceive you as adding something to what I have said, not taking something away from it. We're building on the relationship, developing trust so that there can be a better deal for everyone concerned.

There may be times when you want to use 'but' deliberately, and you need to realise that it will work against whatever has just been said. Sometimes I've opened my mouth and put my foot right in it. Immediately I've regretted what I've just said. By adding a 'but' at this stage I've been able to redirect the rest of the sentence.

NEGOTIATING NUGGET:

When emotions are running high, check the other person's understanding of the issues.

d. Assume you will achieve what you want

Rather than say: 'Are you interested in having this product?' I would say: 'When will you take delivery of this product?'

By the way you use language you can build in an assumption that you will reach agreement. Load your language so that you reach the point where you and I are talking together about being successful. By your language assume that we are going to do business. Talk about *when* we'll do it, not *if* we'll do it.

2. Memories

Many leading psychologists believe that our behaviour is conditioned by our memories. How we behave today is only a reaction to our past experiences. The more you know about people's memories the more you'll understand how they tick.

The strategies people have for making decisions today are based on memories of the past. If you've had good negotiations with someone, you're likely to believe you will have more good negotiations. Excellent negotiators are just like elephants—they have a long memory.

Make sure the person you're negotiating with has a good memory of you. It will stand you in good stead for future negotiations. When that person thinks of you, the memory is a positive one.

3. Decisions

From a very early age we are making decisions about life. Starting as children we gradually create our own map of the world's territory. Our perception of reality is built by the decisions we made in early life and continue to make now.

The man's decision not to put his hand in the fire is based on the childhood memory of putting his hand in the fire and getting burnt. Because of his ability to generalise (see above), he now uses this experience to develop an unshakeable belief that hot things burn.

Remember, though, the map you have created for yourself is not the territory; it is drawn from your experiences of the world at large. The decisions you make about life are likely to be very different from those of other people. The more you know about the way others make decisions the better you are able to influence them. We'll talk about this more in the next section.

4. Perceptions

The perceptual filters are about how each of us perceives the world. They are neither right nor wrong; they just are. Perceptions are often called meta programs because they are metaphors for the way we're programmed.

You and I could look at the same 3D picture. You might see the three-dimensional hidden object immediately while I only notice a series of dots. My perceptual filter is different from yours. The fact that I can't see things in 3D doesn't make me less of a person than you. However, as the curious negotiator that I am, I'll want to find out how you perceive things so I can talk to you in the same language.

By learning how other people handle information through their filter system you can begin to predict their actions. This can help you understand that person's responses better when you are around the negotiating table.

Each perceptual filter has attached to it certain patterns of language. If you talk about the glass being half full, I will, too. In that way I'm talking the same language as you. I'm not right and you're not wrong; it's just that we're different.

I believe there are nine perceptual filters that are particularly relevant to negotiation:

a. Towards/away from

When people talk in terms of their motivation in life they use the 'towards/away from' perceptual filter. The 'towards' person speaks of goals, priorities, to have, to achieve, to obtain. The 'away from' person talks about situations to be avoided, things to be excluded, problems to get away from.

Think of each perceptual filter as a continuous line. At one end you have someone who is completely 'towards' (solution-orientated) and never considers the 'away from' (down side) position. At the other end you have someone who is driven with the desire to get 'away from' (problem-orientated). In practice few people are at the two extremes; most fall somewhere along the continuum.

Most of us in the business world are solution-orientated. Nevertheless if you meet people who are problem-orientated —and my experience is that some buyers have this perception— you will need to change your language to explain how they can get away from their problem. If you are problem-orientated I will want to speak to you in your language even though I am solution-orientated.

It would be nice in life to get people to fill in a form to find out where they are. However, this is not possible around a negotiating table! A simple way to find their towards/away from stance is to ask them something like: 'What would be your ideal job/holiday/car?'

From this you can deduce their towards/away from perceptual filter. For example:

☐ **Towards** = 'My *goal* is to *achieve* success in business—and *get* well paid for it.'

☐ **Towards** with some **away from** = 'My *goal* is to *achieve* success in business—and *get away from* mundane jobs.'

☐ **Away from** with some **towards** = 'I want to *get away from* mundane jobs and *steer clear of* company politics, and I want to *achieve* success in business.'

☐ **Away from** = 'I want to *get away from* mundane jobs, *steer clear of* company politics and *avoid* problems.'

Once you understand their perceptual filter you can load your language around the negotiating table.

b. Sameness/differences

'Sameness' people want the world and everything in it to remain as it is and get very stressed out with changes. They talk about things being the same and things in common. 'Differences' people want the world to change constantly and get frustrated if things remain the same. They use words like new, different and change.

A 'sameness' person will probably stay with the same company for 40 years; a 'differences' person may move on every six months. Unless they have been made redundant, how long people stay in any one job gives a clue to whether they have a 'sameness' or 'difference' filter.

An example of a question you might ask to discover the other person's 'sameness/differences' is: 'How does this product compare with products you've used before?'

☐ **Sameness** = 'This product's the *same* as I've had before.'

☐ **Sameness** with some **differences** = 'This product's nearly the *same,* but there have been some small *changes.'*

☐ **Differences** with some **sameness** = 'This product's *changed* but some of the features are the *same.'*

☐ **Differences** = 'This product is completely *different.'*

And remember that this is still the same product. It's only the other person's perception!

c. Proactive/reflective

Proactive people want to get things done *now by* initiating, jumping in and making things happen. They will use expressions such as 'now', 'done', 'do it', 'get on with it', 'make it happen' and 'go for it'. Reflective people wait for others to take the initiative, consider all the information, are analytical and take their time. They like expressions such as 'understand', 'think about', 'consider', 'could' and 'would'.

NEGOTIATING NUGGET:

Develop good listening and questioning skills.

In conversation a *proactive* person uses many active verbs and crisp, clear sentences. A *reflective* person uses passive verbs and sentences that are long or convoluted or never finished.

One way of finding where a person fits on the *proactive/reflective* filter is to ask: 'How do you go about making a decision?'

☐ **Proactive** = 'I just *know. I go for it.'*

☐ **Proactive** with **reflective** = 'I *go for it* but I *consider* the information as well.'

☐ **Reflective** with **proactive** = 'I like to *take my time* and *consider* the information. Then I *get it done.'*

☐ **Reflective** = 'I need time to *consider* and *reflect* on all the information so I can *understand* it thoroughly and *think about* what we *could* do, and it's then and only then that I'll decide.'

Unlike the other perceptual filters, the *proactive/reflective* filter tends to result in clear polarisation. Woe betide two negotiators at the opposite ends of the line maintaining their own position regardless of the other person's position!

d. Internal/external

Internal people decide for themselves, using their own quality standards. They have difficulty accepting other people's opinions and directions. They use phrases like 'I decided', 'I did', 'I knew', 'I felt good'. *External* people use outside information to know if they have reached quality standards. They need other people's opinions and directions. They talk about 'my colleague supported me', 'my boss agreed with me', 'other people told me'.

Internal people will only be convinced about your product or service if they decide it's what they want. So with them you might say: 'Only you can make this decision.' *External* people will need to get feedback before making their mind up. With them you could say: 'I suggest you ask your colleagues before buying this product.'

You could discover a person's *internal/external decision-making* filter by asking: 'How do you know when you've made the right decision?'

☐ **Internal** = 'I just *know* it's the right product. *Nobody else* will convince me.'

☐ **Internal** with **external** = 'I just *know* it's the right product, but I always *check* with the boss.'

☐ **External** with **internal** = 'Once I've *checked* with my boss, I'll *know* it's the right product.'

□ **External** = 'I'll *ask* the department. Then I'll *check* with the boss.'

And remember the *external* person's motto is: 'I used to be indecisive but now I can't make up my mind.'

e. Impulsive/number of times/every step of the way

The *impulsive* person will be convinced or not by only a small fraction of the information. The person who has an *every step of the way* filter will never be totally convinced and will need detailed information for each small decision made. The vast majority of people who fit in between these two extremes need a certain number of examples to convince us that it's the right decision.

I wish people in shoe shops would take the trouble to find out how many pairs of shoes I need to see before I'm convinced I've made the right decision. It would be easy enough to ask me: 'How many pairs of shoes did you see before you bought the shoes you're wearing?' The answer in my case would be two. The shoe shop that only shows me one pair loses out because I go down the road to see another pair before deciding. The other shop that shows me six pairs gives me far too much information so I walk out before I've made a purchase.

In many organisations people are expected to get three quotations for every job. Three is a common convincer for many people, especially because of the organisational requirement. To find out what is the convincer for a person simply ask: 'How many products did you consider before you made your final decision?'

□ **Impulsive** = 'I just knew.'

□ **Number of times** = 'I considered three products '

□ **Every step of the way** = 'I'm still not totally convinced it was the best buy.'

Finally, a few people need a set period of time before they make decisions. They might say: 'I need to sleep on this and I'll let you know in the morning.'

f. See/hear/read/do

How would you be convinced that a training course would really work for you? Would you need to:

□ See information?
□ Hear information?
□ Read about it?
□ Do it?

NEGOTIATING NUGGET:

Give organisations three options and you will move the odds in your favour.

In terms of negotiation, present the information in the way that other people prefer:

❏ Show them your product
❏ Get them to hear from other happy customers
❏ Let them read a brochure
❏ Let them drive the car or hold the puppy

g. Global/specific

NEGOTIATING NUGGET:

Excellent negotiators express how they feel about things. If they don't like something they'll say: 'I feel you've really let me down there.'

Global people talk in generalisations and concepts, omitting any details. Specific people talk in great detail, losing sight of the overall purpose.

We are having a meeting about cars. A global person might be talking in terms of transportation or even ways to move around. A specific person may well talk about the colour of the paintwork, the headrests and the kind of trim. You can imagine what a challenge it could be for these two people to negotiate!

Diagram 2 shows the various levels on the *global/specific* continuum. You and I as negotiators can disagree about the paintwork, the headrest and the trim, which is the detail. However, we do agree on the concept, which is that we need some form of transport. So all good negotiators start from the point of agreement (transport) and only move down the chart to the detail as long as they can maintain agreement. (For more on this vital topic see chapter 5: 'Listening and Questioning Skills'.)

h. Thinking/feeling

The *thinking* person is logical, analytical, objective and dissociated from the decision-making process. The *feeling* person understands others' needs and values, is interested in persuaded others and is emotionally involved in the decision-making process.

If you want to convince a *thinker*, present your ideas in a logical, analytical way. Convincing the *feeler,* on the other hand, involves empathy and an understanding of the other person's needs and values.

Thinkers

❏ Emphasise the objective and the task
❏ Present information logically
❏ Encourage an 'if . . . then' conversation
❏ Back up your proposals with facts
❏ Refer to, and value, their reasonableness

Feelers

❏ Emphasise the effect on themselves and other people

- ❏ Encourage a conversation around the impact on people involved
- ❏ *Show how their personal values will be met*
- ❏ Show how your proposal will increase harmony
- ❏ Refer to, and appreciate, them for who they are: warm-hearted and compassionate

Existence

Movement

Transport

Specific (details)

Car

Ford

Escort

Global (purpose)

1.4

Ghia

Two doors

Blue

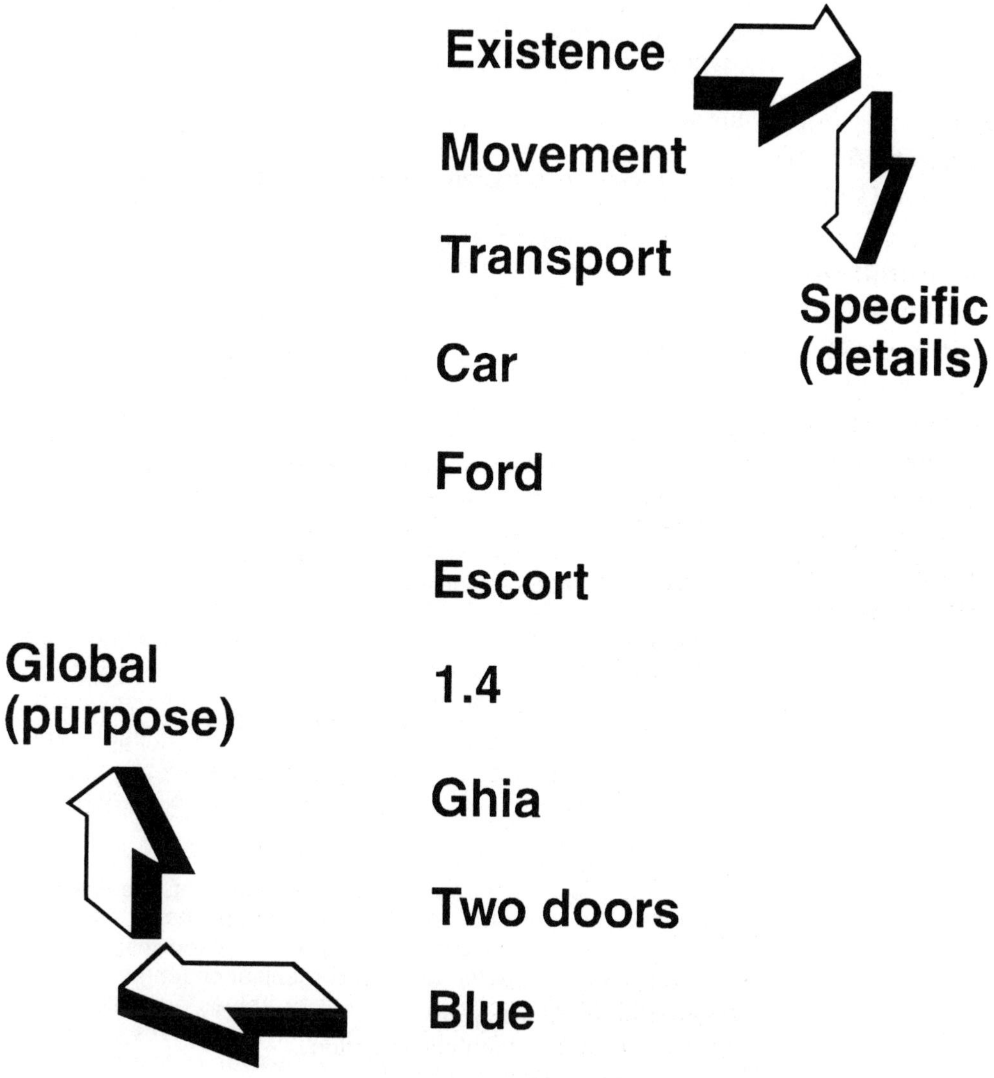

**Diagram 2
Global/specific**

i. Judging/perceiving

Judgers like to make decisions quickly so they can move on to the next task. They are always driven by deadlines and object to negotiations that drag on and on. They are likely to make a decision before they have enough information. Conversely, the *perceiver* can never have enough information to make a decision. When the judger shouts: 'Deadline!' the perceiver replies innocently: 'What deadline?' Perceivers are flexible, adaptable and remain open to change.

Judgers

- ❏ Use a systematic approach when presenting information
- ❏ Provide all the basic facts needed to make a decision
- ❏ Present a plan for implementation
- ❏ Be on time and stick to time
- ❏ Ask for a decision *now*

Perceivers

- ❏ Be more casual when presenting information, going with the flow
- ❏ Expect lots of questions and be prepared with back-up information
- ❏ Show them how your solution is flexible to change
- ❏ Accept that they may need time to make a decision
- ❏ Value their resourcefulness and flexibility

5. Values

Values are motivators. They will energise you to do or not to do things. Find out the values of the people you are negotiating with. Then you can use those values in the language you use towards them. As a result you can show them empathy, respecting their model of the world.

People have a wide range of values. We are talking here specifically about work values. People's values must always be recognised as powerful motivators. During these times of constant change many organisations have shifted their values. Often people are attracted to join an organisation for the values it displays. Over the process of time their values or those of the organisation change. As a result, they find themselves in conflict and suffering stress. A sure way to disaster is to undermine someone's values.

Everyone has different values and it is important to find out what they are. Whatever they are, that's perfectly OK. They are neither right nor wrong. People are not crazy, sick or broke; they're just different.

Finding out people's values is vital to effective

negotiation. One way of discovering the other person's values is by noting clues as the conversation continues. Another approach is by asking questions:

'Is your job an interesting one?'

'Yes.'

(It's important to check that the person is motivated. Otherwise you will not discover their values.)

'Why is your job important to you? It gives you a chance to be . . . what?'

'To be creative.'

'Creative. Is that important to you?'

'Yes. Very.'

'And what else is important to you?'

'To benefit other people.'

'So it's to be creative and to benefit other people?'

'Yes. If it's just making bolts to go in certain holes I'm not interested. I want to do something that will change people's lifestyles.'

'What's wrong with making bolts? Why that sort of thing?'

'It depends what the bolts are for. If it's to make yet another luxury consumer item I'm not interested. What I want is to benefit people.'

'Why is it important that you don't do that kind of job?'

'Because I want to change people through training or writing or whatever.'

'So you want to change people? And you want to be creative in doing it?'

'Yes.'

'And what if you had a job where you couldn't benefit people?'

'I wouldn't stick at it.'

'So if I could help you to achieve your value to benefit people, would you like that?'

'Yes.'

By asking a series of questions I've come to understand your work values:

☐ Being creative
☐ Benefit people
☐ Change people

It's vital that I use precisely the same words you used. The words you use for each of your values can be totally different from my understanding of them (see '1. Language' above).

If I were selling a photocopier to you, based on this information, I would make sure my product's benefits emphasised your values: 'This solution has changed people in other organisations and freed them up to being creative. I know it will benefit your people.'

On this occasion you as the buyer might even pay more for a machine as long as it fulfils your values.

6. Beliefs

Our beliefs are the assumptions we have about ourselves and the world around us. They are our on/off switch for our ability to operate in the world. I believe I'm good at tennis or I'm lousy at it.

Beliefs are subjective and emotionally charged. They are caught in a time warp from when we first made the decision to believe in a particular thing. Beliefs can be either enhancing or limiting.

A friend of mine was brought up in a musical family and told throughout his childhood that he couldn't keep a tune in a bucket. As an adult he held firmly to that belief. One day, convinced that his belief needed updating, he auditioned for a music group and went on to be featured on television and records as a musician. His belief about himself had changed. In the same way, you can change your beliefs about yourself and others. All you have to do is know what you want to believe, and do it!

In negotiation, find out the person's beliefs and you will find the areas to concentrate on or avoid. The successful negotiator works within other people's belief system—sometimes even to change their beliefs—and achieve a better deal for all concerned.

7. Attitudes

Wouldn't it be nice to be able to go up to people and say: 'Right, change your attitude,' and they would? We have little effect on people's attitude. You can affect people with language and they perceive things because you're entering their model of the world. You can't do much about their attitudes. What you *can* change, though, is your own attitude.

I live in the village of Kilsby. We have a bridle path that goes from Kilsby to Crick. It's a pleasant little path and I take my dog along it. You can stop and chew the fat with the occasional local person. It's quiet for most of the year. Then summer comes and the ramblers are out in force.

I was talking to one of the farmers up there not so long ago about all these ramblers. He told me a tale about a couple of them he had met that day. One had come across from Crick and had wandered over the brow of the hill and down to where the farmer stood.

'What are the people in Kilsby like?' he asked.

The farmer replied: 'Where have you just come from?'

'From Crick,' replied the rambler.

'And what are the people in Crick like?'

'Oh, I don't know. Miserable lot. I went into the pub there. Sat in the corner. Nobody spoke to me. Didn't enjoy it. Awful place. Terrible people.'

'Do you know,' the farmer replied, 'you'll find people just like that in Kilsby.'

'I thought so,' the rambler concluded, satisfied.

A few minutes later another rambler came along. He was in the Negotiating Professionals Rambling Club.

'I'm just going down to Kilsby,' he said to the farmer. 'What are the people like there?'

'Where have you come from?'

'I've just come from Crick.'

'What were the people like in Crick?'

The Negotiating Rambling Club member said: 'Fantastic. I went in the pub there and had a drink with some of the locals. What tremendous fun they were! We had a really good time and I enjoyed myself immensely. I enjoyed it so much, in fact, that it was a shame to come away. I knew the rambling club were coming over to Kilsby. So what are the people like here?'

'Well,' replied the farmer after a thought, 'you'll find them just the same as they were in Crick.'

'Gosh, I thought they would be!' exclaimed the rambler excitedly.

There is an attitude of wanton curiosity about things that you should take along with you to all negotiation. And like our rambler you'll find people 'just like that'!

Summary

The fundamental rules of communication are:

❐ Respect the other person's model of the world
❐ Remember that they do things for their reasons, not yours
❐ Communication is the response you get
❐ Feedback is the secret of future success
❐ The negotiator with the most flexibility has the most effect

The communication model can be summarised as follows:

We take in information through our **senses**—what we see, hear, feel, smell and taste.

We then reduce that information down by filtering through our life's experiences: **delete, distort** and **generalise** the information coming in.

At any one time we can only deal with **five to nine piece of information** at a conscious level.

We pass the information through our **filters:** language, memories, decisions, perceptions, values, beliefs and attitudes.

NOTES

That creates an **internal representation** of the event—the pictures in your head and the way you might talk to yourself.

In turn that affects your **state**—how you feel about it. If you have a good picture you feel great; if you have a bad picture you feel lousy.

Those two affect your **physiology**—thinking, feeling, stance.

Your internal representation, state and physiology have a direct bearing on your **behaviour.**

Your behaviour becomes the **input** into the other person. If your input is in a positive way that matches the other person's model of the world then we have good communication.

4
Building
Rapport

As social animals, humans can't help communicating. That's just the way we are. So, the more you can create that social atmosphere of communication in negotiations the more those involved can begin to trust each other. The way to create that atmosphere is through *rapport.*

Rapport is about respecting other people's frame of reference and model of the world. There has been a lot of study of rapport. Much of it has been in the field of Neuro-Linguistic Programming. NLP is the study of what works in the area of thinking, language and behaviour.

As a certified NLP trainer I've been particularly interested in what makes excellent communicators and negotiators. The one thing they have in common is their ability to develop good rapport.

Rapport, in fact, is the foundation of all excellent communication. When you are on the same wavelength as the other parties, the negotiation can be settled quickly and efficiently.

It's important to realise that only a small amount of what we communicate is through what we say. Research has shown that communication is made up of three elements in the following proportions:

☐ **Physiology—55 per cent**
☐ **Voice—38 per cent**
☐ **Words—7 per cent**

1. Physiology

Imagine you're looking around at people in a restaurant. Even though you can't necessarily hear what the people are saying, you'll soon notice which ones are in rapport and which ones are not.

At one table you might notice two men negotiating a deal. One is sitting up, spouting away with wide gestures of his hands. The other is slumped forward, an elbow on the table to support his weary head. He gazes down, swirling the remains of some red wine in a glass. These two people are not in rapport, and the deal

NEGOTIATING NUGGET:

Discover how the other side thinks, feels and behaves and you will soon be in rapport with them.

is probably about to collapse.

At another table two other businessmen are in negotiation. One is leaning on his right arm. You notice the second man is unconsciously leaning on his right arm as if he were reflecting the other's position in a mirror. One leans forward to say something. The other man instinctively leans forward to hear the reply. The second man scratches his chin reflectively. The first man, too, lifts his hand to the lower part of his face.

It's almost as if these two businessmen are partners in the same dance. That's what I call rapport.

The people in rapport are the ones who, without realising it, follow each other's movements, gestures and expressions. People in rapport tend to *match and mirror* each other.

Who follows who? With people in rapport it isn't easy to tell. Rapport happens naturally. By consciously matching and mirroring the other person we can speed up the whole process.

The people in rapport are the ones who, without realising it, follow each other's movements, gestures and expressions

Family rapport has its origins in modelling on one or more people within the family. For instance, I almost know the jokes my brother is going to tell before he tells them.

When I go out for a drink with some close family and friends we all lean forward and pick up our drinks at the same time. It's almost as if someone shouts, 'Go!'—though no one actually says anything. Such spontaneous actions are a good indication of real rapport with others.

You can take this process one stage further. Once you've paced the other person's physiology and rapport has been established, you will be in a position to *pace and lead.* The other person starts to follow your movements and you will be able to set the pace and direction of the negotiation. This is a subtle art that can be practised with everyone you meet until it becomes a natural negotiating program.

Physiological signs to look out for of rapport between people are:

☐ **Gestures—the way they move**
☐ **Posture—how they sit**
☐ **Breathing—its pace and depth**
☐ **Facial expressions—nonverbal communication**

a. Gestures

Gestures can be either *micro* or *macro.* Micro gestures are movements so slight that they are often missed. If you are in rapport with people who have a typical British reserve, they are likely to use micro gestures. People more outgoing and gregarious, as many Italians are, may use macro gestures—waving their arms around.

When you are negotiating with someone whose gestures are very different from your natural ones, this presents a challenge. As a British person used to micro gestures you could match and mirror your Italian counterparts by reflecting back a micro version of their macro movements. It is important to feel comfortable in yourself doing it. Otherwise it will look like you are making fun of the other person. And we know what that does for rapport!

b. Posture

Posture is about how people line up their spine when they are seated. It includes the position of shoulders and head as well as legs, arms, hands and even fingers. The lining up of the spine is the most important physiological sign to look out for. If other people sit slouched, I would slouch with them. If they sit bolt upright in the chair, I would, too.

c. Breathing

At a very deep level people in rapport start breathing at the same rate. They will breathe together either from the diaphragm or from the upper part of the chest. It's useful to remember to get rapport with people who are breathing—it's deadly trying to get rapport with people who aren't!

Of course, you may come across negotiators whose breathing you don't want to mirror. They might have asthma, be prone to shallow breathing or hyperventilate because of agitation or anger. What can you do to develop rapport with such people?

In such cases you could use *cross-mirroring.* You pace their breathing by tapping your finger, for instance. Then, using the tapping, you can pace and lead them to slow down.

NEGOTIATING NUGGET:

People who are like me, like me. By speeding up the process of rapport with someone, you'll find negotiating far easier.

This doesn't always work perfectly the first time you do it. If it doesn't, once again pace, pace and then lead until you've changed the behaviour.

d. Facial expressions

Of the 639 muscles in the human body nearly one in ten are located in the region of the face. Only a few of these are for eating. Most of the rest are for communication of various sorts. Observe facial expressions, mirror them and lead them to a smile.

2. Voice

Mirroring back to the other person can also be through the voice. This of course is vital on the phone, when there is no visual input (see chapter 11: 'Get on the Blower and Blow It'). And we all know how easily it is to be other than totally truthful on the phone.

Mirroring a person's voice isn't a case of meeting a man from Birmingham and talking to him with a Brummie accent— though some of us find that far from easy to avoid at times!

I'm a Midlands person originally, though I spent much of my life in the south of England. I move easily between a Midlands accent and a southern one. Wherever I happen to be, I tend to do that. It isn't my intention. It just happens unconsciously. Now I use it as part of my way of building rapport with people.

The tools I'm presenting to you here will help you gain rapport with people without them thinking you are copying their accent to make fun of them. That would be guaranteed to destroy any rapport built up between you and the other person. Instead, match and mirror people's voices in a way that doesn't appear to mimic or make fun of them. As with physiology you can also pace and lead the other person by the use of voice.

There are four elements to voice:

a. Tone

A person's voice can be high, low or somewhere in between. Mirroring means reflecting back the tone of the other person's voice. To lower your voice you need to speak from the back of the throat—where you gargle. Move your voice back there and you develop a deep, important voice.

There's no point in replying to someone with a deep, important voice using a high-pitched squeaky voice. That's a mismatch. A throaty voice (Edward Heath) and a nasal voice (Ken Livingstone) produce a mismatch. Rapport in such a case is naturally made less easy.

b. Clarity

Some people enunciate their words clearly while others mumble.

If you enunciate each word and the other person mumbles, you have a natural mismatch, and this must be borne in mind when you are negotiating together.

c. Speed

Probably the aspect of voice that causes the most mismatch is speed. Some people talk extremely quickly, others very slowly. The people who talk quickly like to hear others talking quickly. I heard of a managing director who regularly lectured at an incredible speed of over 200 words a minute. In his office he spoke so quickly that slow speakers found him daunting. It was only people who could speed up their speaking to come somewhere near his pace that developed rapport with him.

The beauty of developing rapport with the quick speaker is that you can match his or her pace and gradually slow it down to a more modest speed that becomes acceptable to you both. This pacing and leading must be done subtly. It's a bit like the commentator on horse racing who reaches fever pitch at the end of the race, then slows his voice down gradually, almost imperceptibly.

d. Volume

Some people talk very *loudly* while others talk softly so that it's difficult to catch each word. Matching the volume will ensure that you're both on a level playing field.

3. Words

Although the words themselves are fairly low down the scale of importance, there are important things to be aware of:

a. Key words

People have words that they like. If they like them use them, because you are then talking the same language. Before long, you'll be presenting your ideas in a way that they would present your ideas. You'll talk back to them in their language and, because there's a familiar ring about them, you've developed rapport.

b. Common experience

People normally think of rapport as asking questions: Did you have a good journey? Did you find the place all right? What did you think of the game last night? Although this is only a very small part of rapport, it does have an important part to play.

c. Predicates

Our predicate is our own preference for processing information and the way that's reflected in our language. We take in information through all our senses—sight, sound, touch, taste, smell. We all use all of them. Most people, however, have a preference for one or the other.

In negotiating a deal someone might say: 'It looks right.' In the same situation another person might say: 'It sounds right.' A third person could say: 'It feels right.' A fourth category, the non-specific sensory, is: 'I sense that's right.'

One negotiator says: 'I see that as we look at our vision of the future we can picture . . .' In reply one person might say: 'That doesn't ring a bell with me because it doesn't sound as though that's quite right.' Another might say: 'I can't grasp that. It doesn't feel right and it doesn't move me.' It's almost as if these three people are talking different languages.

Each of us has a preference for sight, sound, feeling or sense. If you notice which one it is in the other person you can adjust your language accordingly. When I'm in doubt I might say something like: 'Let's see what it sounds like and then decide which way we feel we'd like to move forward. If we've got it right then we'll be able to speak about it, see that it's the right way and feel good about it.'

The ideal is to reach the stage where you can move easily to match the other person's preference.

How people are processing information can be indicated by eye movements. If people are looking up, usually they are accessing things in picture form. So you might say: 'How do you see things?' If they are looking sideways they are likely to be processing in sound. So you might say: 'How does that sound to you?' If they look down and to their right, they are probably processing feelings. You might ask: 'How does that feel to you?'

One word of warning: Be careful not to be too pedantic in interpreting eye movements. If in doubt just notice where people's eyes move to when they are talking in pictures, sounds and/or feelings.

Eye movements in themselves can be an intriguing and fascinating area for understanding how the other person is processing information. I can't tell *what* people are thinking; eye movements will tell me *how* they're thinking. This book can only scratch the surface of the subject. I recommend that as you develop your other negotiating skills you study the subject in more detail.

d. Global/specific filters

In the same way that you can pace and lead a person's speed of talking, so you can pace and lead a person's language either upwards to being more global or downwards to the specifics.

Cultivating rapport

Many people intuitively walk into the office and know this is definitely not the day to ask the boss for a pay rise. It is more the day for getting rapport with the boss by pacing and leading. Another day things may be very different. Why? We have an inbuilt sense of rapport. The skill is in cultivating this whenever you need it.

When you meet people for the first time, a good idea is to sit down in the same posture as them. I would go even further in negotiation. Before you go to their office, think about what you wear. If you go to see a managing director wearing a brown suit with a Walt Disney silk tie and he's in a dark grey suit and sober striped tie, you might not fit in and as a result rapport will not be easy to achieve.

After you've met people a couple of times you'll get to know what people wear. Organisations such as businesses and corporations have an unwritten code of standard dress. I spent time training in a very large computer company where white shirts, dark blue suits and sober ties were the order of the day. I could walk around the offices and people thought I was a member of staff because I fitted in with the corporate image they unconsciously wanted to project.

It's not necessary to have a different suit for every person you negotiate with. But be very aware of the kind of person you are dealing with and make sure you take note of both their physiology and the clothes they wear.

The more you can get into rapport with the other person the more you notice shifts in energy. When you're in good rapport you think and feel it's the right moment—and then you know it's time to act.

Times not to act

Much has been written about body language, and there are definitely some clues that will help us to understand how other people are thinking. It's important to emphasise that they are only clues and not absolutes. Before you jump to any conclusion check them out.

Fraud prevention officers are taught to watch for signs of incongruity:

❐ Touching eyes, nose, mouth or side of face may be a sign of lying.

❐ Rubbing hands together is usually a sign of glee and expecting something good to happen.

❒ Signs of nervousness include—sweating a lot, looking around nervously, hands trembling, false smile, feet rooted to the floor, blushing, avoiding eye contact, talking hesitantly, up-and-down voice tone, fidgeting, overly chatty.

❒ Upward movement of the hands is generally a sign of confidence.

❒ Swinging back on the chair with hands behind the head is often an indication of superiority.

❒ Palms facing upwards generally indicates a person who is open and honest.

The thing to remember is that these are only rules of thumb. A man could be rubbing his nose because he is lying, or to give the impression of lying—or even simply because it's itchy.

Summary

Rapport is the foundation stone of all good communication. The process can be speeded up by *matching and mirroring.*

1. Physiology
a. Gestures
b. Posture
c. Breathing
d. Facial expressions

2. Voice
a. Tone
b. Clarity
c. Speed
d. Volume

3. Words
a. Key words
b. Common experience
c. Predicates—sight, sound, touch and nonspecific sensing
d. Global/specific filters

Once rapport is built, the negotiator is in position to *pace and lead* the conversation. If there is any incongruency between the physiology and voice and words, this may be a sign not to take action.

5
Listening and Questioning Skills

What steps can you take to improve your listening skills? God designed us with two ears and one mouth and they should be used in that proportion.

You need to be motivated to listen initially, getting the whole picture before you get into the detail. The only time you speak when you are building rapport is to ask questions.

Understand the other people's model of the world—what aré they after? Be aware constantly of what they are saying and also what they are not saying. This will give you clues to questions you are likely to need to ask later. Let the whole story unfold and avoid interrupting their flow while they are speaking.

Mirroring

Sometimes it's not easy to keep silent when the other person is thinking. You need to be able to stay silent even then. This is particularly difficult for someone who is extrovert in nature.

If you find yourself needing to talk, simply repeat back the last thing the other person said. This is a form of mirroring, which indicates that you are listening and invites the other person to continue speaking.

Undivided attention

In any given time we can absorb far more information than the other person can speak. When the person pauses between words to think, are we concentrating on what is being said or are we letting our minds wander on to the next thing we are going to say? Instead of drifting off into your own thinking, use that time to think of the kind of questions you need to ask.

Make notes as the person speaks. Give the person your undivided attention.

NEGOTIATING NUGGET:

Be an excellent listener and you will become an excellent negotiator.

Separate messenger from message

Remember, it is the message you are interested in and sometimes there's a temptation to merge the message and the messenger. We can be angry about the message yet we don't need to be tough on the messenger.

'Our company won't do that,' says the other person.

I can simply say: 'Typical. I expected that of you. You said you'd do it and you haven't.'

I might be unhappy with the fact that your organisation isn't co-operating but I'm not unhappy with you. So I can be tough on the message but not tough on the messenger.

A better scenario is:

'Our company won't do that.'

'I have to say that I'm very unhappy with your organisation for letting me down. I was led to understand that it would do it.'

In this way I'm taking the pressure off you as the negotiator and putting it on the organisation, where it rightfully belongs. Occasionally, you may be unhappy with the negotiator. Then it's perfectly appropriate to say: 'I feel you've let me down.'

Active listening

Having got rapport with other people it is important that you demonstrate constantly to the other people that you are listening. This is done by smiling, nodding, keeping an open body posture (legs and arms unfolded). And of course, if you have paced and led the conversation, the other people will be smiling, nodding and keeping an open body posture while giving you all the information you need.

Changing from listening to questioning

Once you've listened attentively you are ready to enter the first phase of questioning. This will make sure your understanding of what the other person has said is the same as their understanding of what they've said. This is done by a process of clarifying, checking understanding and reflecting back.

1. Clarify

Make sure you've heard clearly. Ask questions like:

'Would you mind repeating that?'

'Can you clarify that for me so that I can grasp it clearly?'

2. Check understanding

Here you repeat what the person has said:

'So what you're saying is . . .'

'As I understand it, what you've said you would like is . . .'

3. Reflect back

When we reflect back what the other person has said, we seek to understand the logic and the emotion attached to it:

'Do I understand that you're really excited about these concepts?'

'From what you've said I guess you're happy with the proposal.'

Questioning for information

a. Open questions

As part of the listening process you need to ask questions. Once you thoroughly understand what the other person wants in terms of thinking, feeling and behaving, you can move on to ask questions.

Always start with an open question:

'Would you tell me some more about . . .?'

'Explain to me about . . .'

This leads you back into listening and the first phase of questioning.

b. Probing questions

Probing helps you to start uncovering the details of what is being discussed:

'Tell me some more about this particular bit.'

When probing to get more understanding, use the six words that can never be answered with a simple 'Yes' or 'No':

'Who . . .?'
'Where . . .?
'When . . .?'
'What . . .?'
'Why . . .?'
'How . . .?'

c. Closed question

The closed question focuses on clear understanding:

'Is it . . .?' or
'Do I understand it's . . .'

It is always a 'Yes' or 'No' answer and it leads back again to listening. As you go round the circle of listening followed by questioning, you gain a clearer understanding of the issues involved. From time to time you will need to summarise what you've uncovered so far:

'What I understand so far is x and y. Is that correct?'

Think of yourself as a car manufacturer wanting to buy specified ball bearings from me. The first thing I do is listen clearly to what you want, then summarise my understanding:

'So, from what you've said I understand that you're in a phase of growth.'

'Yes, that's right. And I need ball bearings for 12 components in each car.'

'Tell me about each of these 12 components.'

You, the client, give me the information, including sizes and kinds of steel needed.

'What I understand is that you need steel ball bearings with the following specifications . . .' I then outline the specifications clearly before moving on.

d. Summary

There's a need for constant summaries to ensure we are still on course (see Diagram 3). If you are going on a trip in a yacht and you're one degree off course, it might not matter much at the beginning. Yet the further you go on the journey the further you will be from your destination.

An example of summarising is:

'So what we've discussed so far is x and y. Is that correct?'

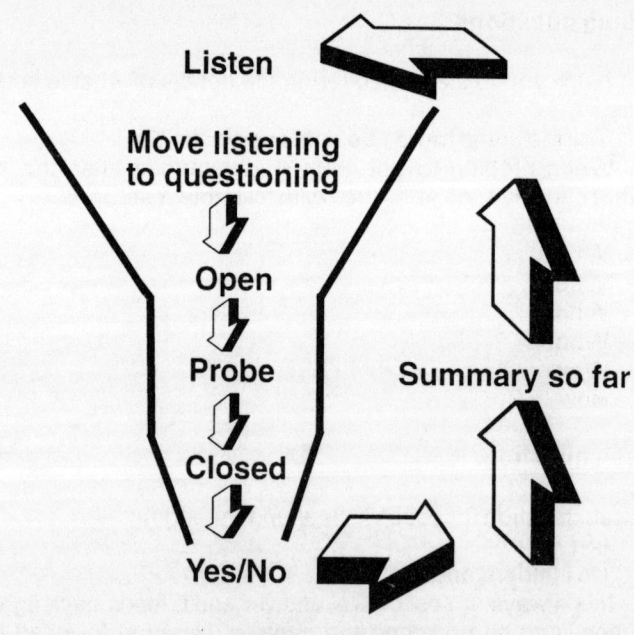

Listen

Move listening
to questioning

Open

Probe

Closed

Yes/No

Summary so far

Diagram 3
The listening funnel

Questioning to get the whole picture

Questioning for information starts at the level where the person is most comfortable (see global/specific filters in chapter 3: 'What Makes People Tick?'). You can then move the questioning up to the purpose or down to the specifics. You can also move the questioning sideways to find comparisons (see Diagram 4).

Two possible questions I could ask to move you from the specifics to the overall plan are:

❐ What is the purpose?
❐ Why are you buying that?

To move you down to the specifics I might ask:

❐ What specifically do you want?
❐ How exactly will that work?

The way to find out information at the same level I could ask:

❐ Is there another example of this?
❐ How does this compare?

By moving the person through all levels you can get an overall picture of what is needed. People have a natural tendency to start at a certain level. As I've already pointed out, some people go for higher abstraction while others want more detail.

When you have rapport with people you listen to them, clarify and respond at their level, then you start to move them up or down the chart accordingly. You and I may not agree on an estate but we could agree that we want a car. There are always levels of agreement. Find those and work from them and you'll be able to reach agreement.

This is the essence of the Camp David Agreement between Israel and Egypt, which I've already mentioned. This process of listening and questioning ensures that the areas of agreement are easily identified.

I have a natural tendency to talk in broad conceptual terms. My colleague is a man of detail. When the two of us are in rapport and have agreed a framework, I'm happy to move down the chart to the minuscule details. Both of us feel good about this process.

If two people negotiating with each other are people of detail there can be a clash because there are more things to disagree with. More and more detail can lead to more and more conflict. If two people operate naturally at a higher level, you may be able to agree the overall aims and the way forward. However, you may be a bit woolly on detail, including drawing a clear contract for the negotiation.

NEGOTIATING NUGGET:

The best place to start negotiating is from a position of agreement rather than disagreement.

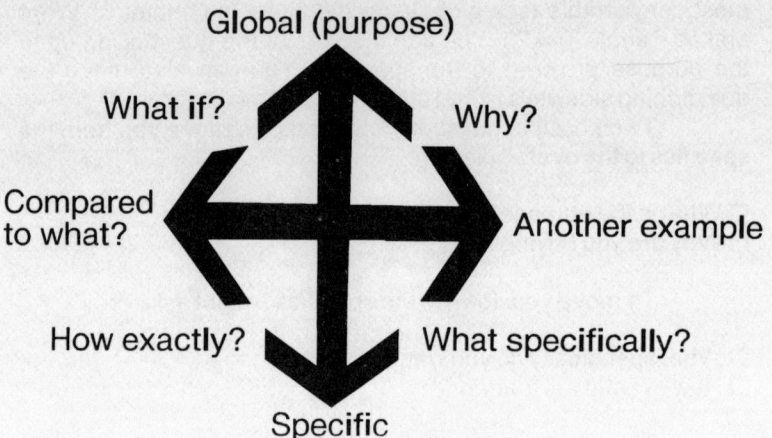

Global (purpose)

What if? Why?

Compared to what? Another example

How exactly? What specifically?

Specific

Diagram 4
Getting the whole picture

NEGOTIATING NUGGET:

Until the final agreement, there's room for negotiation or for backing out of the deal.

When you reach that contracting stage you need to move down to the detail level to get the agreement. You only move down as long as there is agreement. If you start getting into disagreement you need to step back and summarise: 'What we've agreed so far is . . .' It's a constant process of going back up and down until you've dotted the i's and crossed the t's on the contract.

For example, I'm selling you frozen fish products. We get to the point where we've agreed that you are in the business of retailing frozen food. I won't allow you to be specific until you agree that your main business is retailing frozen food. Then we discuss frozen fish.

'Is it a line you do at the moment?'

'Yes. The only problem is that it often has a three-month sell-by date.'

'I realise that could be an issue for you. However, we have come to an agreement that you sell fish.'

'Yes.'

'So what we need to do now is sort out the details of you and me working together and for me to sell you frozen fish products. I realise that three months is a concern of yours. In that case we'll have to make sure that the amount of stock you keep is constantly at a level low enough so that you never meet that three-month sell-by date.'

'Right.'

'What we're after with a contract here is finding ways of

supplying you with smaller amounts more frequently so that the products are constantly turning over.'

'That sounds good.'

The negotiation continues as each layer is agreed. Things have now reached a stage where you have agreed to take four lines of frozen fish products. Now there's a new one that you are reluctant to try.

'In that case there seem to be three options,' I say. (See impulsive/number of times/every step of the way in chapter 3: 'What Makes People Tick'). 'One, you don't take any at all. Two, you give me some estimate of how many you think you can sell. Three, I supply you half of what you think you can sell so that you have plenty of room for a buffer.'

'That sounds really excellent.'

Summary

Listening involves:

❏ Mirroring—repeating back what the other person has just said

❏ Undivided attention—keeping your mind focused on the conversation

❏ Separate messenger from message—directing your feelings appropriately

❏ Active listening—smiling, nodding and open body posture

❏ Changing from listening to questioning
       Clarify
       Check understanding
       Reflect back

❏ Questioning for information
       Open questions
       Probing questions
       Closed question
       Summarising

❏ Questioning to get the whole picture

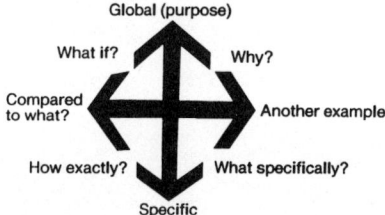

Part Two: Planning

6
Seven Steps to Planning Negotiations

It is vital to plan a negotiation, and there are various levels of planning. At the highest level you are on a journey, travelling from Scotland to the Home Counties. At the other end of the spectrum you might be going from 27 Robert Burn's Row, Ayr, Ayrshire, to 33 Railway Cuttings, East Cheam, Surrey.

Getting lost a few times on a journey soon becomes a great motivator in you deciding to plan your journey. If your organisation can afford for you to get lost a few times in negotiations, this will motivate you eventually to plan. Otherwise, planning every negotiation is absolutely essential.

The map isn't the territory. You sit down and work out the route with a road map in front of you. When you're on the actual journey you may find all kinds of things that change the plan—road works, diversions and traffic jams. Nevertheless, if you have the map to start off with, you can then consider options and other directions should you experience an obstacle.

In the same way that the journey is updated as new information becomes available, the planning for each negotiation needs adjustment as the story unfolds. The plan isn't written in stone; it's fluid and will flow constantly (see Diagram 5).

I've drawn up seven distinct steps for planning negotiations:

□ Define the overall purpose
□ Examine the background
□ Decide the strategy
□ Specify objectives
□ Assess the bargaining power of each side
□ Plan arguments
□ Arrange your team and tactics

1. Define the overall purpose

Ask yourself: 'What am I really after? What am I negotiating about?'

> **NEGOTIATING NUGGET:**
>
> **All the tactics in the world will never replace a good strategy.**

You may start negotiating about a small thing and end up negotiating about something big. For instance, I may be negotiating with you about buying a pen. Yet there may be a lot more to it than just the pen. What I may be after is developing a long-term relationship with you rather than just selling you a pen.

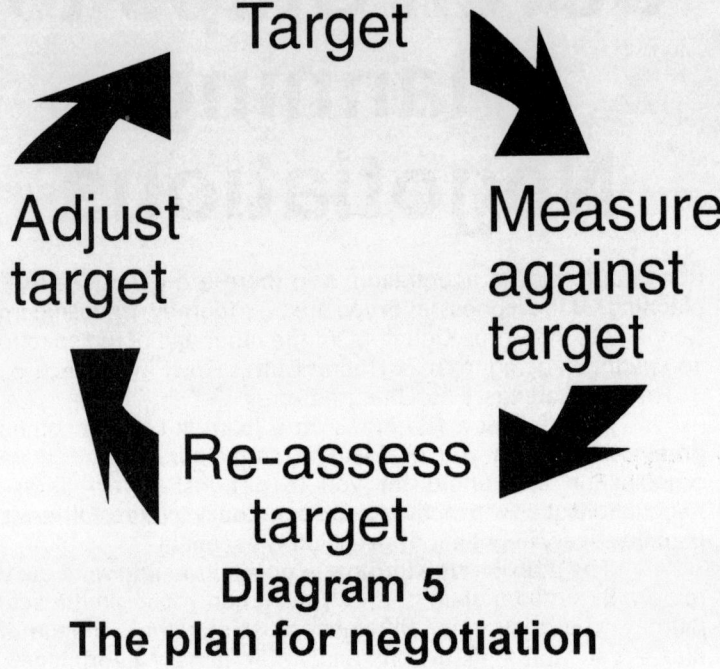

Diagram 5
The plan for negotiation

Remember the five digits in the helping handful? (See chapter 2: 'The Helping Handful'.) Each of these is important here. What might start off with me selling you a pen could end up with my organisation selling your worldwide organisation all the tools you need to communicate. Of course, there will be many steps in between the pen and worldwide communication! This takes us back to Diagram 4.

You may need to ask other questions to clarify your overall purpose. How will you know when you get there? How can you measure how successful you've been unless you have an overall aim?

2. Examine the background

Once you know the overall frame, you can go into the detail of planning the negotiation. To do this you need to look at the background and see how factors in the background affect your specific targets:

a. Put the current negotiation in context

How come you and I are negotiating at this point in time? What information do I have about you and about past dealings with your organisation?

b. What is the history as far as we know?

Find out anything about the relationship between the two organisations in the past. Check previous negotiations and, if possible, talk with the people who were involved. The past has a bearing on the present, though success is by no means guaranteed.

There's no such thing as jam tomorrow. If the other side start to promise things in the future (jam tomorrow) you may need to go back to the drawing board. It you haven't done business with them before, remember that you're setting the precedent for business with them in the future. So remember, if you're cheap today, the other side will expect you to be cheap tomorrow.

c. What are the rules, written or otherwise, and the rituals to be observed?

In international negotiations people spend considerable time negotiating the rules. In the same way, organisations can lay the ground rules before the negotiation starts. Negotiating about the negotiation may include criteria for working, agreeing on the relationship and deciding what happens if there is a deadlock.

If your negotiations take you into another culture, make sure you do your homework in this area

One way of dealing with deadlocks is to agree in advance that you both will put them on one side and continue with the negotiations. The next stage, at the end of the negotiation, is to deal with the deadlock. If that doesn't resolve things, the final stage might be to bring in an arbiter. Of course, it's far better to have negotiating rules in place *before* you get into deadlocks that have to be broken (see chapter 10: 'Breaking Out of Deadlines and Deadlocks').

In western society the ritual may be merely a handshake and offering the other person a cup of tea. In the Middle East, however, rituals may be far more complex and crucial to the negotiation. If your negotiations take you into another culture, make sure you do your homework in this area.

d. What groups are involved or need to be involved?

Consider who is already involved and also who else needs to be involved. Draw up an organisational diagram of the characters involved. How do they relate internally with each other in the organisation? Who in your organisation are the best people to talk to the equivalents in their organisation?

Put the chart on the wall and commit it to your visual memory.

e. Who are the personalities involved?

What do we know about the other people? How do they filter information? What do we need to do in putting our ideas forward in the best possible way so that they understand them clearly? How might we rephrase things using their model of their world (see chapter 3: 'What Makes People Tick?')?

Add to the organisational diagram notes on each person's personalities using Post-it notes or something similar.

f. What is the climate like between us?

Is there likely to be co-operation or conflict? What sort of things are involved in the personalities? What things are going to result in co-operation and what in conflict? It's much better to find places of co-operation—common ground—before dealing with conflict. It's a good idea to have them clearly marked out before you go into the negotiation so you know what you're dealing with.

Finally, collect all relevant information. Get to know as much as you can about the other side.

3. Decide the strategy

Before the negotiators get around the table it is important to decide strategy. There are three main factors to consider here:

a. How can I precondition the negotiation?

What are the advantages/disadvantages of each of us accepting? Can I in some way turn the disadvantages to advantages? What are the advantages/disadvantages of either of us rejecting the negotiation? Can I increase the advantages and decrease the disadvantages to ensure a more satisfactory outcome?

Finally, what is my BANNO (Best Alternative to a Non-Negotiated Outcome)? If I can't negotiate with this person, what alternatives do I have?

b. Can I do this by releasing or not releasing information?

Is there any information that we can pre-release, or are there things already released such as price lists and company brochures? Other things that could be released include budgets, proposals, likely positions and their relative importance.

What can we do to precondition the meeting? How can we gain more information about the other party? What are the advantages and disadvantages of doing this from the three perceptual positions:

❐ From our position?

❐ From the other party's position?

❐ From the position of an impartial outsider?

The person who controls the agenda has control on the power. In certain negotiations I've prepared an agenda and presented it to the people concerned. I've used this to great advantage in structuring everyone's expectations. I've looked carefully at what's on it and in what order. I've also been careful to leave off what I don't want to discuss.

The other party were delighted with the agenda I presented because they didn't have to do any work on it. However, I deliberately put together an agenda in a way in which it made it easier for us all to negotiate. Beware of the temptation to use this as a tactic unethically. You might win the battle, but you'll certainly lose the war.

Within this area it's important to understand each individual's styles and behaviours. In whose court is the ball when you arrive and meet face to face?

In terms of strategy, do you need to negotiate things separately or linked together? Are you looking for a total package or for separate parts? What concessions do you have and what value do those concessions have to you as opposed to the other party?

For instance, if you're buying a computer from me, the value of a manual to you is enormous. The value of it to me may be small. It would be easy for me to give that concession away.

Think strategically. What is the concession worth to me and what is it worth to the other person? This will ensure that you get value exchange. The worth of the concession I'm offering is not what I perceive it to be but what the other person's perceived value of it is.

How can we use the agenda to structure people's expectations of what's going to happen?

c. If we can't agree, can I make sure it costs me less than it costs you?

At first sight this may seem as if I'm aiming at a win-lose outcome, which isn't true. What I'm after is ways of keeping you around the negotiating table long enough for us to find a solution that can benefit us both. The way I can do this is to point out how the disadvantages to you of not doing business with me far outweigh the disadvantages to me.

4. Specify objectives

Having prepared the ground, you now need to be much more specific about what you are after. To measure the success of a negotiation you need to have in your mind three scenarios: the ideal outcome, the realistic outcome and the fall-back position for each item in the negotiation (see Diagram 6).

NEGOTIATING NUGGET:

Decide in advance what you want from the negotiation.

a. Ideal outcome

This is the outcome that is the highest you could possibly dream of getting. You advertise a car for £1000 and someone comes along and offers you that very amount. The deal is clinched yet you somehow feel dissatisfied. The ideal outcome, if realised, leaves people frustrated, wishing they had asked for a higher price in the first place. The ideal outcome is your advertisement to the world of what in your wildest dreams you would like.

b. Realistic outcome

The realistic outcome is what you would expect to get. Realistically, you would hope to get £900 for the car you're selling.

c. Fallback position

When push comes to shove, everything else failing, you would be prepared to take £850 for the car. That's your fall-back position.

The three scenarios need to be linked to your assessment of the bargaining power of both sides and your overall purpose (see above).

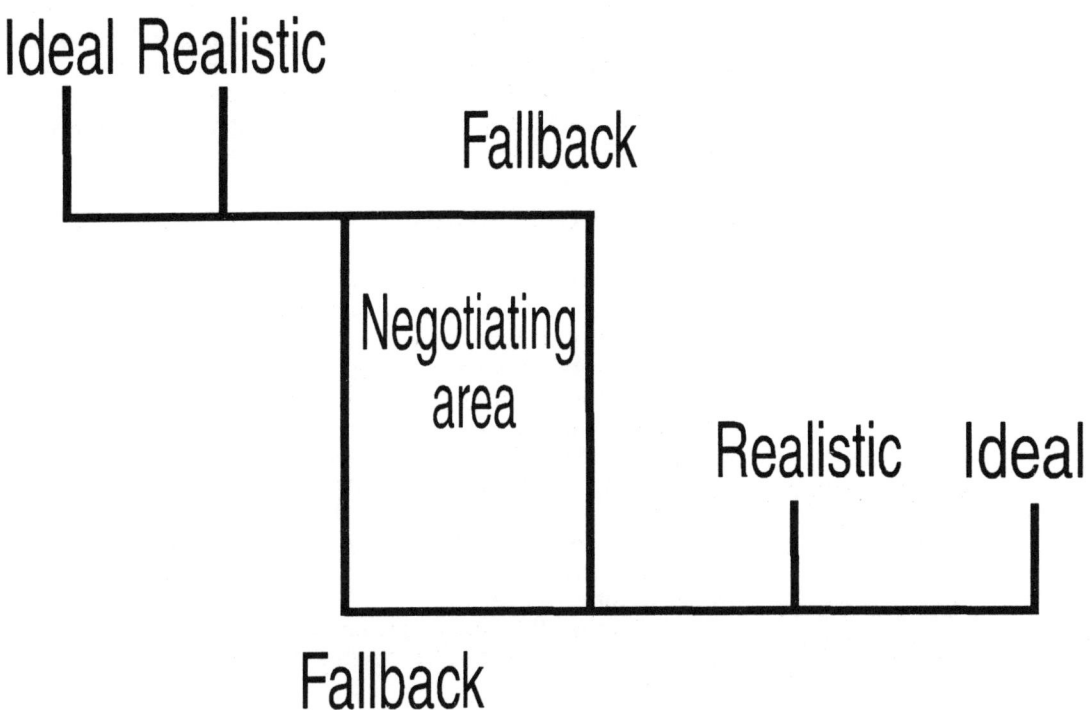

Diagram 6
Specifying objectives

At the same time as looking at the actual amount of money involved, you need to consider how the money is going to be paid. Paying by instalments is not worth as much as cash up front. It's important to set yourself clear targets regarding what you're wanting to achieving. You need to know what you want, what you're prepared to accept and what isn't acceptable.

In negotiations the seller tends to package things together and the buyer always unpacks them and looks at the individual components. Each negotiator needs to be able to look at things both as individual components and as an overall package. This means you can clearly mark out the success level at the end.

Other elements in specifying your objectives are time and delivery.

5. Assess the bargaining power of each side

If you don't consider the bargaining power on each side you might give to the other side more power than is needed.

When negotiators operate as sellers they usually assume that buyers have more power because they can take it or leave it. Even then, however, they need to assess their own power as well. What are the distinct benefits that their products and services offer the customer that shift the power in their direction?

If you are the seller, you need confidence in the integrity of your company and its products. This is far preferable to merely giving things away. If someone gives something away to me it's devalued in my thinking. I believe it's devalued in most other people's thinking as well.

Consider the following questions about bargaining power, thinking of them in terms of the three perceptual positions we mentioned earlier:

NEGOTIATING NUGGET:

Let the other party work hard for every concession.

☐ **What is under offer?**

☐ **What is being proposed?**

☐ **What do you expect to gain by achieving your desired outcome?**

☐ **What will you lose by not getting your desired outcome?**

☐ **What will the other person gain and lose?**

☐ **What will each party gain or lose in this relationship?**

☐ **What are the costs to all parties?**

☐ **How will that affect the proposals?**

☐ **What are the long- and short-term consequences for the outcomes we are thinking about?**

☐ **Having gone through this assessment, are our original objectives realistic?**

It may be necessary to go back to the drawing-board. This is very important because a negotiation that doesn't result in a profit is a total waste of time. There comes a point in a negotiation when it may be best to walk away because the original objective has been totally lost.

Negotiators talk about being the devil's advocate—thinking of things from the other side's point of view. We can take this one stage further in stepping out of the relationship and seeing things from an observer's viewpoint. Use this technique as a negotiator and you will be far better at assessing the bargaining power of each side.

6. Plan arguments

How do we make sure that the people we negotiate with thoroughly understand our point of view and that we thoroughly understand theirs? Again I must emphasise the importance of personality in the people we deal with. The way you put things over is more important than the content! (See chapter 3: 'What Makes People Tick?'.)

a. Collect facts and separate these from mere opinions

b. Identify the strengths of your case

Write down a list of your strengths from the other person's point of view. Then answer the questions from their perspective.

c. Turn weaknesses into opportunities

By seeing your supposed weaknesses as opportunities to enhance the negotiation you can link them with strengths. This will ensure that what is perceived as being a weakness—and very often there's something positive you can actually do about them—can be linked with some strengths.

d. Play the devil's advocate

How will this affect the other side?

A group of us had to agree among ourselves. We then played devil's advocate with each other—raising issues, pointing out flaws, asking difficult questions. By doing this we were armed and ready to negotiate with the managing director and present our proposals. We could counter his arguments because we already

NEGOTIATING NUGGET:

Find out what each side wants and how they will be affected if they don't get it.

had our answers developed. We knew what he was likely to raise and we were ready with our answers.

e. Justify your case by listing the advantages and disadvantages of rejecting it

NEGOTIATING
NUGGET:

Remember
that teamwork
involves
everyone
knowing their
position on
the field.

f. Link arguments together with a common theme

Put three undeniable facts together followed by one idea you are influencing the other person to do: 'You've bought apples, pears and bananas. Therefore, I'm sure you'll enjoy these peaches.' This pattern isn't necessarily logical or rational. However, it moves the powers of persuasion in your favour.

g. Identify potential common ground

Use it or hold it back as a concession for later. Make sure that whenever there's conflict you return to the common ground to ensure that it is repeated and re-affirmed.

7. Arrange your team and tactics

Brief and organise the people in your team who are concerned with the negotiation.
Decide roles. Who's going to do what? Is there going to be a chief negotiator, a person to act as a recorder and another as an analyst? Do you bring in people who are experts in particular areas? Are you going to have an observer? Is there someone who manages the process of preparing for negotiation? This may be someone different from the chief negotiator.

For my money, one of the most important roles in the negotiation is the observer—someone who just sits and watches the proceedings. Very often there is more being said by what people are *not* saying than by what is being said. Chief negotiators are often so involved that they miss a major point. The observer can notice these things.

There is nothing worse than a team giving a mixed message. One member of the team says 'Yes' while another says 'No'. I've seen it time and time again and it gives the impression that these people don't have their act together.

What one person really means is: 'Yes, we can do that, but there's going to be some issue.'

The other person means: 'No, we can't do that, but we'll stretch ourselves and help you by doing it.'

Both mean the same thing yet the initial impact is that these people haven't got their act together. As soon as you're putting up an unsure front to the other side, they'll see through it and use it to their advantage.

It is also useful to agree signals in advance about who talks when. Are you going to signal with your hands, pass notes to each other or say something verbally? For example, you could get the chairperson to summarise the position, then ask for time to consider.

Divide the stages of preparing to negotiate into roles that individuals can focus on, for example, the costings expert and background researcher. It can save a lot of time and duplication.

Brief and organise the people in your team who are concerned with the negotiation

We know clearly and precisely who is the mouthpiece at any one time. If a technical issue comes up, agree in advance that the technical person deals with it.

I've been in a situation where the boss was brought along at the end of the negotiation as a show of goodwill to the other side. Someone casually said to the boss: 'Oh, by the way, can't you do a better deal here?' Because the team hadn't preplanned it the boss has said: 'OK, we'll see what we can do.' I had spent ages getting to this very last stage in the negotiation and, because I hadn't briefed the boss properly, he'd given something away at the very last minute.

We want everyone in the team singing from the same hymnsheet. Just because the boss gets involved doesn't mean he is the chief negotiator. All members of the team need to know where they fit together. It is the chief negotiator's responsibility to make sure everyone knows their role. It's very easy to let something slip.

Negotiating teams need to work well together and could benefit from learning from each other about negotiating skills and team building in a role play before going out for the big contract. You can learn a lot by being in the other person's shoes.

Another important area is to know when to get adjournments. There are times when you as a team need to talk. You've reached a stage where you need to have time out for further discussion. This could be part of the strategy you decide in advance. Make sure you have control and sufficient power.

Summary

1. Define the overall purpose—What am I negotiating about?

2. Examine the background:
- ❐ Put the current negotiation in context
- ❐ What is the history as far as we know?
- ❐ What are the rules, written or otherwise, and the rituals to be observed?
- ❐ What groups are involved or need to be involved?
- ❐ Who are the personalities involved?
- ❐ What is the climate like between us?

3. Decide the strategy:
- ❐ How can I precondition the negotiation?
- ❐ Can I do this by releasing or not releasing information?
   Consider things in three ways:
      From our position
      From the other party's position
      From the position of an impartial outsider
- ❐ If we can't agree, can I make sure it costs me less than you?

4. Specify objective:

- ❐ Ideal outcome
- ❐ Realistic outcome
- ❐ Fallback position

5. Assess the bargaining power of each side:
- ❐ What is under offer?
- ❐ What is being proposed?
- ❐ What do you expect to gain by achieving your desired outcome?
- ❐ What will you lose by not getting your desired outcome?
- ❐ What will the other person gain and lose?
- ❐ What will each party gain or lose in this relationship?
- ❐ What are the costs to all parties?
- ❐ How will that affect the proposals?
- ❐ What are the long- and short-term consequences for the outcomes we are thinking about?
- ❐ Having gone through this assessment, are our original objectives realistic?

6. Plan arguments:
☐ Collect facts and separate these from mere opinions
☐ Identify the strengths of your case
☐ Turn weaknesses into opportunities
☐ Play the devil's advocate
☐ Justify your case by listing the advantages and disadvantages
   of rejecting it
☐ Link arguments together with a common theme
☐ Identify potential common ground

7. Arrange your team and tactics—Decide roles and rehearse
outcomes

Part Three:
The Process

7
The Seven Stages in the Negotiation Process

As an excellent negotiator you will seek to move every negotiation through seven stages:

1. Present Your Ideal Outcome

All sides in the negotiation need to come up with their final goal or ideal outcome: 'This is what we're after.' Whenever you do this you ensure that you justify, clarify, prioritise and answer questions on cost so that it is a well-formed, well-planned outcome. In this way the other people involved in the negotiation will know precisely what you are after.

The way you put forward the proposal is crucial to the negotiation. Excellent negotiators avoid *irritators.* Someone might say: 'Let me put forward this excellent idea.' It might be excellent to him but it isn't to you, so you find it irritating. Or the other side might say: 'This is a fair and reasonable offer.' If may seem fair and reasonable to them but it isn't to you, and you immediately feel annoyed.

Tiny things like that can trap the mind. If you use an irritator the other side only hears that and not the rest of the negotiation.

It is also essential to avoid *argument dilution.* Someone might say to you: 'This is a very good hotel. It has pleasant rooms. The food's delicious. It has ample parking, which is important in the middle of town. The staff are friendly. They've decorated the foyer in pink and green recently. They have an unusual porter system where you have to bleep a certain number.'

By the time the person is finished you are lost in the detail of the decor. Yet the key things for you are that the hotel has a good bedroom, tasty food and ample parking.

As you present your points be careful not to go into too many details too quickly. As we've already seen (see the section

> **NEGOTIATING NUGGET:**
>
> **The art of excellent negotiating is to give only the *key benefits.* The golden number of benefits is three.**

on global/specific in chapter 3: 'What Makes People Tick?'), the more detailed you become the more you are likely to find disagreement. It's a bit like a chain with one weak link. Once that weak link has been found, it becomes the centre of focus and everything else is forgotten.

While you don't need to go into great detail at this stage of the negotiation, it's important to keep in mind what specifically you are after. If you lose sight of your ideal outcome you can end up disappointed and frustrated.

NEGOTIATING NUGGET:

Let the other party make the first move.

I heard of an office manager back in 1973 who was negotiating with a carbon paper salesman. As the negotiation progressed he got caught in the trap of progressively increasing his order because of the better and better discounts on offer. By the time the deal was agreed he had bought huge quantities of carbon paper.

After the carbon paper was delivered, the shocked typists reminded him how much of the product they used. He then worked out that he had been sold 40 years' supply of carbon paper— enough to keep the office running well into the next millennium. The trouble was that within 15 years, with the advent of cheap photocopying facilities, carbon copies were being phased out in almost all offices.

There are no good strategies to overcome lousy planning. The office manager forgot his ideal outcome in his effort to get something as cheaply as possible, He ended up with a lifetime's supply of something he didn't really want. The result was a lose-lose outcome for everyone as he would never again buy office supplies from that particular company.

There are no good strategies to overcome lousy planning

2. Listening, Signals and Asking Questions

As an excellent negotiator you need to listen to what the other people are saying. Listen so that you understand their position. Read between the lines for any *hidden signals* they may be putting out. Typical hidden signals you might pick up on include the following:

Overt Message		Hidden Message
'We don't normally give discount'	=	'We'll give you three for the price of two'
'We never give discount as large as 10 per cent'	=	'We'll give discount of up to 9.99 per cent'
'I won't go a penny below £90,000'	=	'£90,000 is the opening bid'
'I'm not authorised to go below this price'	=	'Talk to my sales manager'
'These are the standard terms'	=	'Let's talk about a variation'
'At this stage we're not prepared to discuss this matter'	=	'Let's negotiate this tomorrow'
'We'd find it difficult to supply you at this price'	=	'Difficult, but not out of the question'
'The best we can do at the moment'	=	'We'll do something later'
'We couldn't produce that amount in that time'	=	'Let's negotiate on price, delivery, quality and quantity'

NEGOTIATING NUGGET:

Plan strategies to get out of a negotiating meeting. This will give you time to think.

Acknowledge the signals given by the other party. Signals need a signalled response. Ask plenty of questions to clarify your understanding of their position. At the same time, give out your own signals in the conversation. Be prepared to signal your willingness to move into a negotiating position.

At this point you need to start exploring the proposal from as many different angles as possible. Ask questions to help you find the global picture (see global/specific in chapter 3: 'What Makes People Tick?'): 'What's the overall purpose of this?' Get to the specific details by asking: 'What specifically are you after?' Staying at the same level you could ask: 'Is there another example of this?' (see Diagram 3 in chapter 5: 'Listening and Questioning Skills').

Before you move on to stage three, it is important that both sides have presented their ideal outcomes, listened to each other and asked questions to clarify points. Only then can you move on to the next stage:

3. Amend the Proposal

Many proposals need some form of amending. The way you make those amendments can either enhance or destroy the good relationship you have built so far with the other party.

You and I are negotiating. You ask me lots of questions so that you understand fully my position. You then put forward a great idea that I don't particularly like. The danger is that I could quite easily come back and say: 'No, that's not a good idea' and then propose my idea.

How would you feel about that? Pretty awful, I would guess. I've effectively said: 'Your idea's a load of rubbish and mine's really good.' You might respond: 'No, forget that. Let's do it my way.'

Suddenly, like two wrestlers, we're caught twisting each other's arm, desperate to move things to our own advantage. This is the first place in a negotiation where a deadlock is likely to occur (see chapter 10: 'Breaking Out of Deadlines and Deadlocks'). The proposal/argument/counter proposal spiral can go on and on with things getting increasingly out of hand. We are stuck in an attack/defend deadlock.

The proposal/argument/counter proposal spiral can go on and on with things getting increasingly out of hand. We are stuck in an attack/defend deadlock

It's important to amend the proposal—and it's vital to amend your language. (Notice the word 'and' rather than 'but' here.) You need to change the way the proposal is presented by adding, not taking away. Two key words here are 'if' and 'then': *'If I did this, then would you be willing to do that?'*

Suppose I'm buying a house from you. Your price is £100,000, which is considerably more than I wanted to pay.

I say: 'If I pay £100,000, then would you leave the carpets and curtains?'

This is not an offer. I'm merely inviting you to think through a possible amendment. It's important not to give concessions at this stage; they are more appropriate for later on in the negotiation.

On the other hand I might say: 'If I can complete in three weeks, then would you reduce the price to £95,000?'

Should the other party get angry or defensive at this stage, you are perfectly in your right to say: 'Wait a minute. We haven't made an agreement. We're just exploring.'

'If' and 'then' are wonderful words that you can do a lot with. When a person says yes to an agreement, that isn't necessarily the end of the negotiation. That's really the beginning of finding ways of fulfilling it.

The alternative approach is direct bargaining. I say to you about your house: 'No, £100,000 is too much. I can offer £95,000.' This gets us both into the attack/defend position, which as we've seen can be counter-productive.

These first three stages of the negotiating process are all about finding out and respecting the other person's model of the world. Step one is when you've put forward the idea. In step two you've asked questions and clarified what's gone on, sending and receiving unspoken messages. At this third stage, the amendment stage, you receive questions from the other party so that you can explore their position.

You as an excellent negotiator can ask questions about their position: 'Why do they need to go lower?' 'Are they on a limited budget?' The other party, too, may need to ask further questions so that they are clear about your position.

By the end of this third stage you've come to understand each other's position. Now you're ready to get into true negotiation.

4. Packaging

In the packaging stage you seek to match the needs and priorities of the other party. This includes matching their interests, needs, priorities and other things that are of value to them.

As an excellent negotiator you will constantly ask the question: 'Is there any way I can rejig or repackage things so that both parties get a better deal?' For instance, payment or delivery terms can be changed to meet the needs of each of the

NEGOTIATING NUGGET:

Remember: Nothing is agreed until you get to the final contract.

companies concerned. The result is that both parties benefit from the package.

It's important here to understand the other party's needs and values. This isn't about conceding anything; it's about repackaging the proposals to suit all parties concerned.

Our deal may be over different coloured pens. My normal offer is a pack of three pens—one blue, one red and one green. If your need is 50 per cent blue pens, and I can work that so there is no loss to me or you, then both of us will be happy.

Think of another scenario. The negotiation is around cases of frozen peas. I normally sell frozen peas in batches of 1000 cases. You don't have room in your freezer for the full 1000 cases. You start to amend the proposal by saying that you'd be happy to buy 1000 cases of peas as long as I could arrange the storage space.

Because our relationship is based on trust, I've already explored this issue. I've done my homework and know that you have a high turnover of peas and will sell them in a reasonable amount of time. However, what you don't have is the freezer space out the back to carry them.

NEGOTIATING NUGGET:

Remember to keep the deal open as you might narrow your room for bargaining later in the deal.

I amend the offer in such a way as to benefit you. 'What if we deliver them in two halves?' I suggest. We haven't made any concessions here but we've managed to get around the original obstacles and now both parties are happy.

What does this mean to you? Do you see it as a concession? In terms of value to you, it is worth a lot. It is, in fact, added value. So I'd want to get something back for it. This leads naturally into the next section:

5. Bargaining

I can now ask you to make a move: 'If we deliver the peas in two lots of 500, then would you buy 250 cases of frozen carrots?'

Having given a concession to you I am looking for something in return. In the packaging phase we were talking about things that didn't cost either of us any money. Here we are talking about concessions that cost money. I say here: 'I've given you something in the bargaining process and I want something in return.'

The important thing is not the cost of the concession to me but the value of it to you. The fact that our warehouse would be empty if we sent you all the peas is irrelevant. Although it doesn't cost me much, the storage space is very valuable to you.

You might then say: 'If you supply half the peas as well as the carrots, then would you give me a discount of 20 per cent?'

I might reply: 'We're not in a position to offer you 20 per cent.'

That, of course, is a hidden message meaning: 'We can offer you something.'

I can then respond with something like: 'If you take the

frozen peas and carrots, we'd be willing to give you 100 cases of broad beans.'

So the process of bargaining goes on. We go through each of the items in the negotiation. We return regularly to packaging because packaging and bargaining are interlinked and there is what I see as a 'process within the process'.

NOTES

NEGOTIATING NUGGET: Always remember when negotiating: If you shoot from the hip you're likely to end up with a bullet in your foot!

The important thing is not the cost of the concession to me but the value of it to you

Think of the first five stages of negotiation in the following way:

Part One: We understand each other's model of the world

☐ The proposal comes up
☐ We listen to the proposal and ask questions to understand the other person's point of view, listening for any hidden messages
☐ The proposal is amended, giving the original proposer a chance to understand the other party's point of view

Part Two: The core of the process

☐ Packaging
☐ Bargaining

As long as you've done your homework and are well planned, keep rapport with the other side and manage to go through the first four stages, you enter the crucial bargaining stage of the negotiation with good will. You will then find ways of getting through it.

Bargaining is the second place where deadlock may sometimes occur. As long as you've traversed any deadlocks at the amendment stage, the chances are you'll be able to get through this stage, too, and find ways of making the outcome successful for all concerned.

Remember again, that there is no agreement until it's all over. Having an 'If . . . then' on amending proposals and in the bargaining process makes sure that the deal isn't finalised until it's agreed.

In the bargaining stage it's important to get all the items of the negotiation out on the table before you make any concessions. Make sure you understand the other person's point of view. Don't get 'picked off' item by item. You might then run out of ammunition and will not be able to close effectively. Make any settlement on each item conditional on the whole negotiation being accepted.

6. Closing

Closing the negotiation is the central part of the process. The purpose of closing is to make sure you have an agreement that all parties are happy with. There comes a time when 'If . . . then' becomes so refined that it's self-defeating.

The first question is: 'Have we got all that's on offer?' Assuming there's more, if you keep going will you be able to get it? Is it worth trying to get that extra?

In my early days I became so zealous I'd spend hours negotiating in a market for things that only saved me a few pence. That in itself became extremely useful practice when I came to negotiate for hundreds of thousands of pounds. Now I don't bother about bartering in a market all the time. The professional negotiator realises that time is money.

The temptation in any negotiation is that you're having such a good time bargaining, packaging and finding different ways of doing the deal that you forget to close. You could be in danger of reaching another deadlock because you haven't closed. Avoid this deadlock by closing as soon as possible.

Another important element of closure is to make sure you've noted down what the issues are and have ticked them off as you agree them in a way you've both understood. Highlight the concessions given and the benefits of what has been agreed.

There are several ways to close:

❏ **Summary close**
The simplest way to close is to say: 'Let's summarise what we've agreed.' If you've taken notes, this makes a summary easy to do.

❏ **Concession close**
There may be a need to make a small concession at the very end to get agreement. It's an excellent idea to keep this concession up your sleeve until the last minute. It might be of little value to you, but it may be very important to the other party.

☐ Assumptive close

Once all the stages have been completed you can say: 'Shall we sign the agreement now or later?' This is based on the assumption that the deal has been agreed and that you are both ready to sign. It shifts the other party away from any further discussion about the negotiation. It is the old sales strategy of saying: 'Would you like six cases or 12 cases?' rather than merely saying: 'Would you like to place an order?'

7. Contracting

The contracting stage is the most dangerous one of the whole process. At each stage it's easy for things to be misinterpreted. Now we've agreed, perhaps even shaken hands, euphoria sets in. Whoopee! We've done it! That's the time when things can go wrong.

It's important to keep calm, be clear what has been agreed and get things in writing. In the closing stage make notes. At the contracting stage people think it is such hard work to write things down. The other person might put the wrong interpretation to the contract.

I suggest that the best negotiator always volunteers to be the one who writes down what has been agreed. Of course, with larger contracts things may have to go to the legal department or other parties may need to be involved. What I'm emphasising is that before you leave the negotiating room, both parties have a written copy of what has been agreed. Later, when you talk about the negotiation, it is absolutely clear and there is no comeback, misinterpretation or misunderstanding.

When everything is in place and signed by both sides, you can open that bottle of champagne and celebrate

Not until things are written down in a contract can you say you've agreed. I want to emphasise again that the contracting phase is the place where, in the euphoria of agreement, things can be completely misunderstood. Twenty-four hours later, when you pick up the phone and speak to each, what *you* understood about the negotiation is totally different from what the *other person* understood.

Get your legal department to check everything before finally putting pen to paper. Then and only then, when everything is in place and signed by both sides, you can open that bottle of champagne and celebrate.

Summary

What's on offer:
1. Present the ideal outcome
2. Listen carefully for all the information, including hidden signals
        —ask questions
        —give your own hidden signals
3. Amend the proposals as necessary
        —continue asking questions

The core of the process:
4. Packaging—finding new ways of presenting the product or service
5. Bargaining—concession making

Ensuring a successful ending:
6. Closing and making sure agreements are sorted out
7. Contracting to ensure that all parties know and understand precisely what has been agreed

8
The Top Ten Tactics

Tactics are to the negotiation what silicon chips are to the computer. They are the techniques used at the operational level to bring about a successful negotiation.

Silicon chips on their own have little function. Connect them to the computer's motherboard and they work to your advantage. A good set of tactics without an overall negotiation strategy will never achieve the desired outcome. As a negotiator, you need to have in place a good strategy before trying out any tactics.

While there are both good and bad tactics, in the wrong hands any tactic can become a game-playing technique that is working towards one-upmanship. Such tactics are always unethical and are never appropriate for the excellent negotiator who wants to move towards a win-win outcome.

Hundreds of tactics have been identified. I've chosen a selection of those that are the most used. My purpose is to help you to identify each of them and how they can be countered if necessary. Here, then, are my Top Ten Tactics:

1. Good Guy, Bad Guy

The *Good Guy, Bad Guy* tactic is popular on TV police and detective programmes.

There's a dimly lit, smoky interrogation room in a busy New York police department. The one light in the room shines directly on to the suspect, the criminal who hasn't yet admitted to his crime. There are two other people in the interrogation room, both detectives in plain clothes. One is giving the suspect a really hard time, firing question after question, accusation after accusation, not letting him think straight.

Then, suddenly, the Bad Guy marches out of the room leaving the suspect on his own with the other detective, the Good Guy. This detective sits down opposite the suspect, pours him a coffee, offers him a cigarette and is generally nice to him. The suspect's defences are down and before long he spills the beans to the Good Guy. The tactic has paid off.

In negotiations *Good Guy, Bad Guy* works only with certain people. You sometimes come across someone who is a tough negotiator, very resistant, who won't give way a centimetre.

NEGOTIATING NUGGET: There's power in limited authority. Even the managing director of a company can get out of sticky corners by having to talk first to his production team or accountant.

You probably feel like a criminal because there's this one person grilling you, giving you a hard time, making your life a misery. Then he leaves the room and you immediately feel much more relaxed.

Now it's the Good Guy's turn. He becomes friendly with you, chipping in with some sort of minor concession. You in return spill the beans by making a major concession to him. What would have been a win-win situation becomes a win-lose situation—and you're the loser.

NEGOTIATING NUGGET:

Don't get excited about an agreement until it has been written down or some other contractual arrangement has been made.

With Good Guy, Bad Guy, what would have been a win-win situation becomes a win-lose situation—and you're the loser

If you as the negotiator ever feel like playing this trick on a client, remember that it's unlikely the client will ever want to do business with you again.

There's another version of *Good Guy, Bad Guy.* The person you're negotiating with is the Good Guy and he tells you all sorts of stories about the invisible Bad Guy, who's the boss or someone else in his organisation. This Bad Guy is tying his hands so he can't reach any deals without checking them out. That can, of course, be genuine and it's down to you to find this out. The way to do that is to ask questions.

The negotiator might say: 'I want to help you but my boss has tied my hands behind my back. Maybe you could help me, because I really need to sort this out with my boss.'

The more you know about the organisation and who makes the final decision the more control you can have. By asking good, probing questions you'll discover what's really going on— you'll know if there's a genuine need to talk to the boss or if this is merely a clever tactic.

Another important thing is to look at the characters involved. The Good Guy will tell you about his Bad Guy boss. Instead of merely accepting his word for it, use questioning skills to find out the extent of the boss's power.

Counter measure

The counter measure to *Good Guy, Bad Guy* is very simple. You just don't take the bait or play the game. Don't get sucked in. Recognise it as a tactic and you won't be tempted into giving things away.

2. Taking It Higher

Authority can be used as a negotiating tactic. 'I need to *Take It Higher.*'

It wasn't many years ago that in Communist states across Eastern Europe there was only one person who had power; everyone else was powerless to make the final decision. That was, in fact, a good negotiating position. No one could agree a deal without having to go off and find out about it.

At the other extreme are those people with total power. This worries me. A person in that kind of position can make dangerous mistakes.

Most people have a measure of authority somewhere between these two extremes. Some people can vary the level of their authority to suit the circumstance.

It's useful to decide how far you'll go in offering concessions by limiting your authority as a deliberate tactic. This will stop you giving things away. 'We can only do a discount of £1000. Any more than that and I'll have to talk with my boss. My hands are tied,' you say, knowing full well that you could give a £1500 discount. You have agreed with someone in advance what limit you will go to before *Taking It Higher.* That other person is usually your boss or line manager.

This gives you a good way of getting out of being cornered.

In Taking It Higher someone says: 'I'll have to talk with my boss. My hands are tied'

Counter measure

A counter measure to *Taking It Higher* is to challenge it on the spot.

A person says: 'I can only give you £1000 discount. Any more than that and I'll have to talk to the boss.'

'OK,' you say. 'Can you talk to the boss now?'

If it's a tactic, the other person will fudge this.

Another counter is to say: 'OK, if you can't offer this discount, who can? I'd like to talk to him now.'

Remember that keeping rapport with the other person will allow you to ask direct questions without causing the other person to feel threatened.

3. The Nibble

NEGOTIATING NUGGET:

At the moment when you are most vulnerable, *The Nibble* is often introduced. So be prepared to nibble back!

The Nibble is one of the better known tactics. My wife is brilliant at it, so each day I can watch an expert at work! *The Nibble* comes in at the very last moment when you think you've agreed a deal. At that split second of euphoria *The Nibble* comes in.

My wife and I bought a new sunbed one August at the height of an exceptionally hot British summer. We went to a local garden centre and there were two left. One had a crack in the plastic and was reduced by 10 per cent to £70. We decided to have the one without the crack.

When we got to the till, just as we were paying, my wife pointed out to the checkout girl that there were some scratches on it. This was 7.30 at night and they closed at eight. They wanted us out of the way as quickly as possible so they could begin closing. The manager was summoned and immediately gave us £10 off.

My wife then checked the mattress and—lo and behold—she found a thread loose on that. The manager was again summoned and without looking at the mattress reduced the bill by a further £5.

So we ended up with the best of the two sunbeds at the cheapest price—all because my wife put *The Nibble* to good effect.

The Nibble can be applied in a large deal to buy a major computer network with six terminals. Just as the other people are walking out of the door after clinching the deal to buy the network you say: 'Oh, and by the way, with our current system we have 12 PCs linked into the network. We'd expect you to throw in the other six PCs free.'

I have a friend who used to live in Hong Kong. Whenever you buy a suit in Hong Kong you get a free tie. That's standard business there. When he came back to the UK he had somehow forgotten that this practice didn't happen here. So just as the shopkeeper was wrapping up the suit he'd say, 'Oh, and by the way, which free tie am I going to get with the suit?'

Despite lots of hesitation on the shopkeeper's part, he

was successful in getting his free tie because the deal had gone so far down the line. His suit was wrapped up, the bill had been printed out, though not paid for, and he was ready to leave. So it was difficult for the shopkeeper to back down.

Done with integrity *The Nibble* can be used to great effect. Learn the skill of this tactic on a negotiating course and start putting it into practice even in large stores. You'll be amazed how much money you start saving. Remember, if you get enough nibbles in life it's almost like a proper meal.

Done with integrity The Nibble can be used to great effect

Counter measure

The counter to *The Nibble* is quite simply: Nibble back. For every concession the other people demand through *The Nibble* ask for two in return.

'Certainly, sir. We'll give you a free tie—as long as you buy two shirts to go along with your suit.'

4. Red Herring

Throwing in something that is totally irrelevant can be an effective tactic. If you've got something you don't want to discuss and you have two hours to clinch the deal, you can throw in a *Red Herring* and spend an hour and three quarters making out some part of it to be terribly important. The result is that the main issue doesn't get tackled.

My company was buying a photocopier and we had specific requirements for the machine. The photocopier sales-people spent much of the negotiation time telling us about the add-ons, including sorters and staplers, when what we wanted was a basic workhorse that would last a long time without a great deal of maintenance. The one thing they usually 'forgot' to mention was that their machine didn't come with a service contract. Even though one machine was apparently cheaper, when you took into account that it didn't come with a service contract it was more expensive.

It is easy to get caught up in a price for price comparison and miss the important issues. One company said: 'Did you know that the rival's product counts two impressions when you photocopy an A3 sheet? Our service agreement is more expensive but it saves you money in the long run.' While I don't believe in doing down another company, I appreciated hearing that. We had nearly been caught by a *Red Herring* because we rarely use A3 paper.

If you've got something you don't want to discuss, throw in a Red Herring and the main issue doesn't get tackled

Counter measure

The counter to the *Red Herring* is to say the person: 'This aspect of the product appears very important to you. Let's put it to one side and sort out all the other things first, then return to it at the end.' That keeps the other person on track. If the other person becomes insistent about avoiding the main points of the negotiation, then it will be clearly exposed as a *Red Herring.*

5. Put It in Writing

When people in Britain want to avoid negotiation they *Put It in Writing.* Go into Marks & Spencer and there will be a ticket on a garment for £20, so you pay exactly that amount. There aren't many people who go into Marks & Spencer—or any other store—and negotiate over the price. I'm convinced, though, that you can negotiate the price in quite a number of stores.

The same principle applies to mainstream business. Companies produce catalogues with products and services at a stated price. It's the stated price, so what is the price people pay? They simply pay the price listed. Putting the price in writing is a negotiating tactic that works very well because few people negotiate.

I was asked to tender for a major training programme with one of the UK's largest retail companies. I put in my tender with my price and so did two other tenderers. I found out later that mine was the most expensive of the three tenders.

Fortunately, it met their requirements so they wanted to use my services. They took up my tender because I listened to them and to what they wanted. What I designed was exactly what they wanted. I would much rather make sure that the quality of work people get is what they want, even if it costs them more. Most people will pay a bit more to get what they want.

Because I *Put It in Writing,* they were willing to pay the higher price. They did, however, come back to me and ask: 'Can we do something about the price?' Even by giving a small discount I was twice as expensive as the other two. Yet they were still keen to take up my tender.

In the end I was delighted because I got the contract. They were delighted because they paid less money than the price in writing. And we developed a long-term relationship that still remains.

Once two sides have agreed a deal who puts it in writing? Usually the other side is happy to leave it to you. To ensure that the two parties don't distort their understanding of what's been agreed, make sure it's *you* that put it in writing so that what has been agreed at the end is exactly how you remember it. *Putting It in Writing* also makes sure that you put over your point of view.

NEGOTIATING NUGGET:

Always offer to put things in writing.

Put It in Writing is a tactic that works very well because few people negotiate a fixed price

Counter measure

Remember that *Putting It in Writing* is a tactic and doesn't necessarily mean people won't negotiate on the price. If there's a price in writing, it's usually negotiable.

6. What If?

What If? is a very effective tactic from the buyer's point of view. The buyer keeps saying things like: 'What if we do this?' and: 'What if we do that?' This puts sellers in the position of having constantly to re-examine what they are offering, checking the numbers, the delivery, the production and everything else. If used frequently, *What If?* eventually grinds down the seller.

A salesman is offering me a computer for £1000. The normal delivery time is seven days and the standard payment terms are 30 days. The computer comes with a certain amount of software installed on it already.

Using this strategy I would start asking questions: What would happen if I didn't have the software because I've already got it on another machine? Could that reduce the price or would I get it earlier because you wouldn't have to load it?

What happens if I didn't want it for another month? That would give you the extra time you needed to load the software. How much could you reduce the price?

If I paid you cash up front and didn't have the software on it, what difference would that make?

What happens if I buy a printer with it as well as not having the software on it and paying it with cash?

If used frequently, What If? eventually grinds down the seller

The buyer runs through so many permutations that the sales people get completely bogged down. Before they know where they are going, they are giving things away without realising it.

Counter measure

The counter to the *What If?* tactic is to make sure you as the seller have done your homework. Think things through from the buyer's point of view. A useful approach is to play a kind of devil's advocate in your head, going through the various possible *What If?* questions and permutations. This will make it less likely that you'll get caught out.

The longer a buyer/seller relationship continues the more the relationship falls towards the seller. From the buyer's point of view, therefore, it isn't advisable to stay too long in a relationship because gradually the seller will get to know more about you: your personality, your organisation, how you negotiate competitively, how you find agreement by co-operation.

7. A Bridge Too Far

A Bridge Too Far is another widely-used negotiating tactic.

In chapter seven I used the illustration of selling your house for £100,000 and including the carpets and curtains in the price. Realistically you could expect to get £95,000 and if you desperately wanted to move you'd be willing to accept £90,000.

Supposing I suddenly come in with a bid of £70,000? That's *A Bridge Too Far.* A bridge would be something like £93,000, which would be within the bounds of negotiation. *A Bridge Too Far* is so far away from the original that it goes beyond negotiating into the realms of the ludicrous.

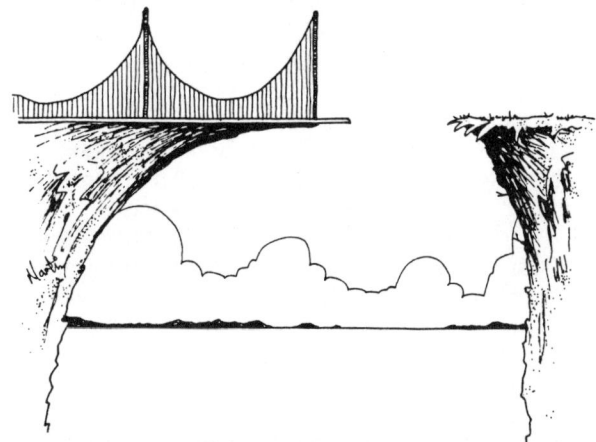

A Bridge Too Far is so far away from the original that it goes beyond negotiating into the realms of the ludicrous

You might reply defensively. 'I wouldn't accept £70,000 under any circumstances,' you say. 'The absolute lowest figure that I'd accept would be £90,000.'

Like it or not, we're now into negotiation! You've now mentioned your lowest figure. I say: 'OK, I'll meet you half way with £80,000.'

You're now miles away from what you were originally after. Yet you've found yourself discussing a deal that you would never have dreamed of discussing before. *A Bridge Too Far* has changed your aspirations.

A Bridge Too Far can, of course, be a very high or a very low figure. The Americans call this tactic *Highballing* or *Lowballing*. Whatever its name, once you go along its route you are in for a lose-win outcome, with you as the loser.

Counter measure

The counter to A Bridge Too Far is to be firm. 'No, my price is £100,000.' Be tough with the other person. As soon as you start conceding on *A Bridge Too Far* you are in danger of falling headlong into the cruel rapids below. Make sure your bridges are well supported.

8. Funny Money

Funny Money is a way of dressing up money so that it doesn't look as much as it is. It's a tactic that confuses the other party by playing with figures.

I needed to buy a new car. I had narrowed the field down to two cars I was looking at. The price wasn't a lot of difference between the two. The deal hinged on interest rates under the loan deals on offer. When it came to the final clinching of the deal, one company offered me 0 per cent finance over two years and the other charged 15 per cent over two years.

When I sat down and worked out the prices over a two-year period, there was about £2000 difference. The argument I heard was: 'Ah, yes, but it's only a few pounds a week.' It sounded very plausible. Yet when I looked at the cost of buying the car over 24 months I realised there was a difference of £10,000 and £12,000. Far from being a few pounds a week, that's *Funny Money*.

I heard recently about a man selling his house for £50,000 plus a free lottery ticket every week for the full 25 years that most mortgages run for. It sounded a good concession at the time, but when I sat down and worked it out I realised that all he was offering was £1300 over a 25-year period. That's *Funny Money*. I'd far rather have £1300 cash in hand now. After all, what is £1 going to be worth in 25 years' time? That £1300 will be decreasing in value over the time. And if you took £1300 off your mortgage now, what difference would that make over the 25-year period?

Newspaper advertising sales people often use *Funny Money.* You book a semi-display space at a cost of £100. They say: 'That's 10 per cent discount for a first-time advertiser.'

That of course comes to £90. 'Can I get any other reductions?' you ask.

'We're doing a special rate of 10 per cent off all advertising at the moment.'

'Great.' You now think you're paying £80 for the advert. The truth is the 10 per cent is off the £90, giving £81. 'Any more?'

'Because you're taking a series of ads we'll give you another 5 per cent.'

What you think is a straight 25 per cent discount giving £75 is ever decreasing, so the advertisement actually costs you just short of £77. Ever-decreasing discounts. That's *Funny Money.*

NEGOTIATING NUGGET:

Never take the first offer made. Imagine, for instance, that you advertise a car for £1000 and someone comes along and says: 'That's great—here's £1000.' How would *you* feel?

Funny Money is a way of dressing up money so that it doesn't look as much as it is

Counter measure

Funny Money tactics need to be countered head first: 'Please tell me exactly how much this is going to cost.'

9. You Must Be Joking!

Every negotiator has seen *You Must Be Joking!* used as a tactic. As you present your proposal, the other side shake their heads, wince, look shocked, draw in their breath sharply and say: 'You've got to do better than that!' It's such an obvious tactic that it seems difficult to imagine anyone falling for it. Yet many people do.

Salesman: 'So this is the laptop computer that meets your

specification. The cost is £3000.'

Customer with shocked look: 'Whew! That's expensive. You must be joking.'

Salesman: 'Well—er—that'll include software already installed.'

Customer shaking his head: 'That's really disappointing. Surely you must be joking.'

Salesman (panicking that he might lose the sale): 'Well—er—we could include a free modem . . .'

You Must Be Joking! is such an obvious tactic that it seems difficult to imagine anyone falling for it. Yet many people do

NEGOTIATING NUGGET:

Get something for everything you give.

A far better scenario is the 'give away' approach:

Salesman: 'So this is the laptop computer that meets your specification. The cost is £3000.'

Customer, smiling: 'Wow! That's fantastic.'

Salesman: 'To ensure you really get the most from your laptop I'd suggest you buy some software. We've got a good deal on offer at the moment . . .'

You Must Be Joking! can come up at any point in the negotiation and can be directed at any of it. Beware of getting caught out. Remember, every time *You Must Be Joking!* is used, it lowers the other person's aspirations. The successful negotiator is after a win-win outcome while this tactic turns it into a win-lose one.

Counter measure

One of the most effective counter measures to *You Must Be Joking!* is silence. Once buyers have said: 'You must be joking' or something similar, leave a silence as if you're waiting for them to finish their sentence. Most people will add something that will then help to open up the discussion again. If you can't manage to hold the silence simply restate your position until you can open the discussions again.

Another useful counter measure is to ask for details of why the offer doesn't meet the other person's needs. Give the other side the concession of free information.

By mastering these counter measures the successful negotiator will not give too much away too soon.

10. Eating an Elephant

A person can do anything—given enough time. Michel Lotito of Grenoble, France, popularly known as Monsieur Mangetout, has eaten his way into the record books since he was nine. His ability to eat metal and glass has secured a unique place for him in the Guinness Book of Records from when it started. Since 1966 he has eaten 18 bicycles, 15 supermarket trolleys, seven TV sets, six chandeliers, two beds, a pair of skis, a computer and a coffin, handles and all. Most amazing of all, he ate an entire Cessna light aircraft. How did he do it? Slowly!

In the same way, *Eating an Elephant* is simple enough. How do you do it? Slowly! *Eating an Elephant* is a tactic in which a person slowly 'eats away' at the negotiation.

I want to buy a stereo system. I say: 'If I buy the whole system from you, will you give me an extra 5 per cent?'

'Yes, OK.'

'If I take a demonstration model, will you give me another 5 per cent?'

'OK.'

'Oh, but it's got a bit of a scratch on it. Will you give me another 5 per cent?'

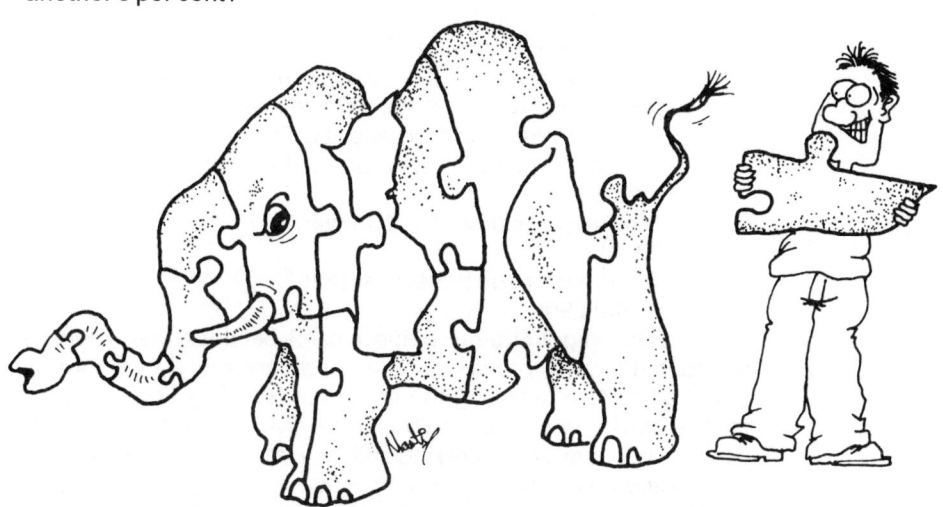

Eating an Elephant is a tactic in which a person slowly 'eats away' at the negotiation

Gradually you take pieces of elephant until you've got exactly what you want.

There's a numeric progression in *Eating an Elephant.* You go from 5 per cent discount, 10 per cent, 15, 20 and what's next? 25 per cent.

Counter measure

Countering *Eating the Elephant* is relatively easy. Agree diminishing discounts such as 5, 7 then 8 per cent rather than 5, 10 then 15 per cent. This sends out a psychological message: 'We're running out of anywhere we can go with discounting. There isn't any more to be had.' This is the ever-decreasing counter to the tactic.

NEGOTIATING NUGGET:

Never negotiate for anything you are desperate for—get someone else to do it for you!

Another variation of the counter goes as follows:

'Can I have 5 per cent discount?'

'I can only offer you 3.'

'How about 4 per cent then?'

'I'll have to go away and think about that.'

A few days later I come back: 'You know your offer of 4 per cent? I'll meet you half way with 3½ per cent.' I've now shifted the odds in my favour.

Let's imagine you're buying something from me. You as the buyer know that people give discounts on the product.

You start off: 'This automatic stapler sells at £100.'

You say: 'You've got to do better than that.'

'OK, £90.' I know I've got plenty of profit at that price.

'You've got to do better than that.'

'£80.'

'You've got to do better than that.'

'Call it £70.'

'You've got to do better than that.'

'£60.' By now my profits have been eaten away.

Let's replay the same scenario again:

'This automatic stapler sells at £100.'

You say: 'You've got to do better than that.'

'OK, £95.'

'You've got to do better than that.'

'£91.'

'You've got to do better than that.'

'Call it £90.'

The negotiation is being closed because there doesn't appear to be any more discount left. It means more profit for me, at the same time allowing the buyers to feel they have won. Of course, buying a stapler at £90 is one thing. Imagine this tactic used in negotiations involving millions of pounds. I know one organisation used this tactic and made a very large amount of money. The buyer was given the discounts he was after but they were hard won and much less than allowing the elephant to be eaten piece by piece.

Summary

1. Good Guy, Bad Guy—avoid getting sucked in

2. Taking It Higher—challenge it on the spot

3. The Nibble—demand two concessions for every one given

4. Red Herring—set it on one side

5. Put It in Writing—if there's a price in writing, it's usually negotiable.

6. What If?—think through possibilities from the buyer's point of view

7. A Bridge Too Far—be tough with the other person and hold your ground

8. Funny Money—counter them head on

9. You Must Be Joking!—one of the most effective counter measures is silence

10. Eating an Elephant—agree ever-diminishing discounts

9
Black Belt Techniques

In this chapter we look at ways of dealing with the aggressive negotiator. How can you defend yourself when the person you are negotiating with becomes aggressive?

If you were to have a black belt in judo or karate the one thing you wouldn't do is use force against force. The black belt expert has the skill to take the force and aggression of an opponent and use the energy to turn the situation around.

In the context of negotiating, you can turn the energy of the opponent to the way you want it. Every statement or question used against you can be turned around to your own advantage, getting over the messages you want to convey.

Notice I use the word 'opponent' here for the first time in this book. The reason is that, even though you and I are committed to a win-win outcome, not everyone else is. Some people are looking to cut themselves a deal by cutting you out. The aggressive negotiator is trying to beat you down and take advantage of you. That negotiator will use every trick in the book to nail you down.

The aggressive approach is yet another form of tactic that needs a counter-measure. I believe it is worth a chapter in its own right because it turns up so often.

Be alert and listen for clues to aggression. The others don't have to shout and bang the table. It can be done so subtly you almost miss it.

One of the classic ways this can happen is by a sudden surprise. Out of the blue they will throw in a hand grenade by applying some sort of pressure that you had no prior knowledge of.

You are selling some consultancy and everything is neatly agreed—or so you thought. You've been lulled into a false sense of security. Then the attack starts.

'Oh, yes, and by the way, we want your consultancy report within 24 hours.'

'Well—er—I'm not sure we can do it in that sort of time,' you reply.

'So you're saying you aren't skilled enough and you don't have the right sort of computing power?'

'Y-e-e-s. Our computer can cope with the sort of thing you want here . . .'

NEGOTIATING NUGGET:

Make sure you get a concession for every concession you give.

'So you're really saying you don't have the skills.'

'Well—er, um—we do have the skills . . .'

'So what sort of problems do you have, then?'

'Er, um, er . . .'

'Look, if you can't do it in 24 hours, you'll need to come down 50 per cent.'

Er, help! you cry inside.

NEGOTIATING NUGGET:

As an excellent negotiator you will realise the futility of mere arguments.

This is a classic way that an aggressive negotiator can spiral your defences down with a series of hand grenades. All of a sudden, you're giving things away just to take the heat off you.

How can you be prepared for this type of onslaught? The best way is practice, practice, practice. If you've ever met people who have a black belt in one of the martial arts you will have noticed that there's something in their behaviour that signals: 'Don't mess with me!' They don't go around looking for trouble, but when trouble arrives they know instinctly what to do.

Get into a positive state of thinking, feeling and behaving:

❑ **Sit up straight**

❑ **Keep your confidence—make sure you are well anchored (this is well documented in most books on NLP)**

❑ **Look the other person straight in the eye**

❑ **Slow your voice down**

❑ **Add more authority to your voice by talking further back in your throat**

❑ **Speak to the other person directly**

❑ **Avoid any weak qualifiers—hopefully, maybe, perhaps, possibly, etc**

❑ **Counter any untrue statements**

❑ **Make sure you get your point over**

The above list is aimed at a Western business situation. Bear in mind that different cultures will have different behaviours, so check before you negotiate.

There are several strategies for handling aggression:

1. Call the other person's bluff

One way of dealing with the hand grenade is to pull the pin out and throw it back! Reply clearly and firmly:

'Wait a minute. I had no idea you wanted it in 24 hours. Our normal turnround time is seven working days.'

2. Withdraw

A second way of tackling aggression is withdrawal. Get away from the force of the explosion and avoid being cornered:

'I've decided that I'm unable to make this deal. Thank you for your time.'

It's important when someone is being aggressive not to be verbally walked over. The other person will pound you by trying to interrupt you in the middle of sentences. This is what politicians often do. Be firm and get your point across.

You might say: 'Hang on a minute. Let's get this straight.' Then go on to clarify the issues.

Once you get on to the slippery slope when the person knows you have been 'got', you will be pushed harder and harder. That's when you need to bring in your black belt techniques.

One way of dealing with the hand grenade is to pull the pin out and throw it back!

3. Divide and conquer

One of the classics of the person who uses aggression as a tactic is to make a statement and then ask a question. If you answer the question, by default that statement stands as fact.

For instance, I might say: 'We all know your company has trouble delivering things on time. The one question I do want to ask you, though, is: "Are you likely to give me a discount on this product?"'

Your immediate reply might be: 'No, we certainly don't give discounts.'

What you've allowed to slip through is a statement that you have trouble delivering on time. If that's untrue it needs countering. Here is a better reply:

'Hang on a minute. That's two things you've just raised. First, our company's record on delivery is second to none. Second, we don't give discounts—and we can, I'm sure, help you in other ways.'

The secret is: divide and conquer. It's very easy to let a statement slip by because the question is so juicy you forget the first statement. If you do that your opponent is likely to come back with something like: 'Wait a minute. You've already agreed that your company has trouble delivering things on time.' The trouble is that, by default, you've already agreed. It's too late to make amends.

4. Keep things simple

When you're facing aggression it is very easy to fall back on jargon because you are then on safe ground. If I'm pressurising you and you talk back in jargon that I don't understand, it could make me even worse. By being 'clever' with me, you end up irritating me even more.

The rule here is: No jargon. Keep things simple and easy to understand. Use facts and information that can be understood by anyone. Break things down into manageable bite-sized pieces.

I once had a man on one of my courses who said his warehouse was 60,000 square metres.

'I don't understand that,' I said. Because I don't think in terms of square metres—or square yards, for that matter—to me it was jargon.

He looked around the room we were working in. 'Well, it's about 400 times the size of this room.'

That didn't help me either—and I told him so.

He thought for a few seconds longer, then came up with the answer. 'It's about the size of six soccer pitches.'

At last I could imagine how huge his warehouse was.

The next step is to discover how to take things that are likely to be jargon and put them into straightforward language that someone will recognise and relate to.

5. Avoid defence

Certainly there's no need to defend your product or service when you're under attack. I might say your product is rubbish.

'No, it's not rubbish,' you say defensively.

'Yes, it is.'

'Oh, no, it's not.'

'Oh, yes, it is.'

Far more than just a pantomime chant, this form of attack-defence-attack is the start of a downhill spiral in our relationship.

When someone criticises or rubbishes your product or service use your adult thinking and rise above the bait. Here is a better scenario:

'Your product's rubbish.'

'Wait a minute. Let me explain to you the benefits of the product...'

Speak in positive terms about the benefit.

Further along the scale of criticism, someone might say: 'I'm not happy with the product.'

Your reply could be: 'What specifically do we need to sort out to ensure that you have all the information you need about our product?'

In this case the person isn't totally happy with the product. Give any specific information needed. A vital part of negotiation is giving the other side time to find out about you, your attitude towards them, your organisation and ways of co-operating with you. It may not seem like that at the time. Even aggressive questioning is often little more than an effort to gather information.

When you are confronted with aggression, see it as an opportunity instead of a threat. Use your black belt skills to turn it around and deliver the messages you want to deliver. When emotion rears its head, ensure that you keep your thinking cap on. Remain detached.

NEGOTIATING NUGGET:

If someone calls your product rubbish, avoid repeating the word 'rubbish' back. This will only reinforce the argument.

6. Plan your strategy

In my early career, after I'd been to a meeting, I would walk down the corridor and suddenly stop and hit myself on my forehead as yet again I realised I'd forgotten a major piece of information during the negotiation. This is a classic case of lack of good planning.

You've been into a meeting and had a great idea. The meeting got a little heated, and you put across your point of view. Only afterwards do you realise that, in the heat of moment, you left out three of the five things you were going to say.

Always plan in advance what messages you want to deliver (see chapter 6: 'Seven Steps to Planning Negotiations'). Use the other side's aggressive questioning as a springboard for delivering those messages you want to get across. Make sure you tell the whole story.

It is vital to write down the messages you want to convey in the meeting. Whatever happens, make sure at some point you mention them.

7. Take time to listen

NEGOTIATING NUGGET:

Leave the other side to let off steam. Sooner or later the kettle will boil dry.

There's nothing wrong with pauses and remaining silent while the other side rant and rave. Pauses are important when you are under pressure. Take time to listen—and to think. Develop good listening techniques (see chapter 5: 'Listening and Questioning Skills'). Take time away from the pressure of the negotiation to think about what has been said and how you can reply to it.

Silence is golden, however long it lasts. While you are silent the other person may well start talking again and might even give something away.

8. Keep on track

When you are being pushed by someone who fires question after question after you, it's very easy to get shunted off into a siding or thrust into a dark alley. We saw the danger of side tracking in the section on Red Herrings in chapter 8: 'The Top Ten Tactics'). Being pushed into a dark alley is a form of side tracking that can be even more scary. After all, there might be a corpse down there.

The way to deal with being pushed into a dark alley is to answer the side-track and redirect the conversation. This technique can work well. There is a danger, though, in using it to extremes, as politicians are good at doing. However, it can also be used positively to get the negotiation back to the point at issue. Take the question, answer it and tag on the end of it the messages you want to get across.

For instance, towards the settlement of a deal for supplying photocopy paper, the buyer says: 'So what plans does your company have for new products next year?'

'That's interesting, and I'd like to discuss it with you sometime. Now, let's get back to this matter of delivery of the paper . . .'

It's useful with this type of aggressive questioning to learn how to do it in a classroom situation before you have to face the full force of it in the negotiation.

Conclusion

In conclusion, remember that the black belt expert never hits back but redirects the other person's aggression to achieve the desired outcome. Follow these three tips and you'll be able to achieve a win-win outcome for all concerned:

1. **Know what you want to say.**

2. **Whatever the other side says—fact or emotion—deal only with the facts.**

3. **Answer the question and ensure that you sell the benefits of whatever your side of the negotiation's about.**

Summary

Get into a positive state

- ❏ Sit up straight
- ❏ Keep your confidence
- ❏ Look the other person straight in the eye
- ❏ Slow your voice down
- ❏ Add more authority to your voice by talking further back in your throat
- ❏ Speak to the other person directly
- ❏ Avoid any weak qualifiers—hopefully, maybe, possibly, perhaps, etc
- ❏ Counter any untrue statements
- ❏ Make sure you get your point over

Ways of handling aggression:

1. **Call the other person's bluff**—pull out the pin and throw it back

2. **Withdraw**—get away from the force of the explosion and avoid being cornered

3. **Divide and conquer**—always answer any statement made just before a question is asked

4. **Keep things simple**—avoid jargon and break things down into manageable bite-sized pieces

5. **Avoid defence**—use your adult thinking and rise above the bait

6. **Plan your strategy**—write down the messages you want to convey in the meeting and make sure at some point you mention them

7. **Take time to listen**—while you are silent the other person may well start talking again and might even give something away

8. Keep on track—answer the side-track and redirect the conversation

Tips to follow:

❏ Know what you want to say

❏ Whatever the other side says—fact or emotion—deal only with the facts

❏ Answer the question and ensure that you sell the benefits of whatever your side of the negotiation's about

10
Breaking Out of Deadlines and Deadlocks

Deadlines

Deadlines in negotiation swing between two extremes: those that are immovable and those that are totally on the move.

1. Fixed deadlines

At one end of the spectrum are the deadlines that can't under any circumstances be moved. It's coming up for the end of your financial year and we both want the negotiation out of the way by then. That is an immovable deadline. There's nothing I can do to change it.

I need to make decisions based on the fact that the deadline is completely immovable. It may not be the perfect deal, yet it is the best deal we've got. The deadline is looming up—and a bird in the hand is worth two in the bush. I have a fixed reference point.

2. Deadlines on the move

The other extreme is a bit like the number 73 bus—there's always another one coming along in ten minutes' time. Deadlines come and go.

In Bosnia the deadlines for ceasefire came and went. I don't know how many times the United Nations and then NATO set ceasefire after ceasefire. There was always a scramble for ground just before the deadline—and the deadline got moved yet again.

3. Flexible deadlines

Between these two extremes are a wide range and type of deadline.

The first thing to do in every negotiation is to check out that the deadline you've been given really *is* the deadline. Allow some flexibility in your planning for fallback. I might tell you I need to fill my diary for next year by October, knowing full well that it doesn't have to be done until November. I've got a bit of flexibility and I can allow things to slip a little.

NEGOTIATING NUGGET:

Remember that deadlines themselves can often be negotiated.

Deadlines on the move are a bit like the number 73 bus—there's always another one coming along in ten minutes' time

One of the interesting things I've noticed over years of negotiating is that the majority of the actual negotiation happens at two minutes to 12 o'clock. In other words, things get sewn up just before the deadline. This is like the situation in Bosnia, where the two sides scrambled for land just before the deadline. It's the *negotiation before the negotiation.* Each side wants as much as possible with which to negotiate.

The deadline itself is a negotiation. The scramble for land just before the deadline is so that the two sides have more concessions to play with.

4. Negotiated deadlines

I take the view that when there is a deadline it should be fixed. This needs to be understood by both parties. The war in Bosnia could well have gone on for ever. NATO enforced deadlines: 'We've got to get an agreement by . . . If we don't get that agreement, the consequences will be . . .' Deadlines must be kept to and the consequences of breaking them brought into force. Otherwise there is no negotiation.

There are four questions to consider when thinking about deadlines:

a. What deadlines am I setting, or is my organisation setting, that are making my negotiating harder than it need be? This may mean reviewing our internal negotiation and all the people involved with that.

b. Is it possible for me or my organisation to extend the deadlines we are proposing? What are the costs and benefits involved in that?

c. What sort of pressures does the person I am negotiating with have from his or her organisation or external pressures (for example, government legislation)?

d. Is there anything that I or my organisation can do to help relieve the pressure on the other side?

The one good thing about deadlines is that they commit all parties to action.

Deadlocks

Deadlocks can actually be good for you! When you are in a deadlock it tests each party's resolve and willingness to stand their ground. Because of this, deadlocks can be seen, not as an end to the negotiation, but as time for a break from the negotiation.

You and I have been going along together in the negotiation and we've ground to a halt. There's nowhere else to go. Getting into a deadlock is easily done. We can become so caught up in developing a close working relationship that we end up not seeing the wood for the trees. It's time for finding another way of approaching the situation.

There are several ways of breaking out of deadlocks:

1. Limit your power

One way of breaking out of a deadlock is to tell the other party: 'I'll have to check that out with my boss.' As we will see in chapter 13: 'The Power Balance', there's power in limited power. Contacting the boss is one way of getting out of a negotiation if it has become stuck.

Another related way is to ask for a five-minute break to get your thoughts together and possibly to contact your boss. You can use this strategy to avoid a deadlock that you see coming up.

NEGOTIATING NUGGET:

If you get stuck in negotiating, ask: 'Do you have the power to close this deal?' If the other side takes offence, say: 'I was only asking.'

2. Make a hot-line call

A second way out of a deadlock is to make an on-the-spot call to someone in your organisation to discuss the matter. This could be your boss or someone in the organisation with an area of expertise. That person might be able to shed fresh light on the difficulty.

It's also possible occasionally to make a hot-line call to thin air. Once or twice I've phoned up 'the boss' when there was really no-one on the other end of the line. I haven't used this as some kind of tactic or dirty trick. It merely gave me breathing space, time to think before I got into the details of a deadlock.

Space to think can help to make sure that when you open your mouth you don't put your foot in it. Without time to think there's the danger of killing off a negotiation. It's far better to think through how you will get out of deadlocks you see looming up.

3. Change the time or money

NEGOTIATING NUGGET:

Excellent negotiators know when it's time to call it a day with a particular organisation and hand things over to another negotiator.

Another way out of deadlines is to go back to the deadlines and see how these can be changed to find different ways of bringing the deal to a close.

You can't move Christmas, of course, but if you have a major order coming in you could change the deadline on a machine I'm supplying to you. Suppose you want two machines—one in two months' time and the other in three months. It may be that I can supply one machine in a month and one in four months' time. Although this doesn't exactly fit your plans, it will give the production you need to meet the demands your customers are making on you. The deadline is broken and we are back into negotiation.

Similarly with money, there's an almost endless list of ways of paying for things: cash up front, part payment, 30 days, 60 days, leasing, half up front and nothing to pay for two years. By changing the way money is paid you may well break the deadlock. This approach comes into packaging and bargaining—finding ways of moving the money around to fit in with your company's cash flow (see chapter 7: 'The Seven Stages in the Negotiation Process').

Suppose you are buying a machine from me that needs to have a service contract. You are limited in the amount of money you can spend in terms of capital expenditure. However, your maintenance budget may not be stretched to the full. There may be some way we can break this deadlock by me reducing the price to you of the machine and putting more money on the mainten-ance contract. Overall, we are still working on the same financial numbers. Yet the new deal fits in better with your organisation's requirements of you to keep within a capital expenditure budget.

A word of warning is needed here: Make sure the change of money is not funny money (see the section on 'funny money' in chapter 8: 'The Top Ten Tactics'). In order to avoid 'funny money', we need to work closely together to overcome a deadlock such as this, which has been imposed by your organisation, not by you.

4. Change the negotiator or team

A deadlock can occur when you and I don't get on for some reason. There may be a personality clash, or it may simply be that we've been negotiating together for too long. Perhaps we've been negotiating with each other 17 times each year for six years and we're now rubbing each other up the wrong way or the whole process has lost its sparkle.

When things reach this stage it is probably time to change the negotiators. You go or I go, or both our organisations change the negotiating team. Fresh eyes can seek out new ways around the issues.

Once the change is agreed, we could enter a dangerous time. Our egos could well be dented. One of us could agree to something we're not happy with just to get through and make it work this time. It is far better to hand things over before this happens.

5. Bring in the specialist

Another way of breaking deadlocks is to bring in someone from the organisation who can speak with authority on an issue that is causing deadlock. If there is a technical problem, it could be worth bringing in an engineer from both sides. The two of them could then work to resolve the difference and the negotiation could be completed.

Bringing in the specialist broadens the team and deals with issues that you or I may have forgotten about. With me in sales and you in purchasing, we may have been caught up too much in the figures. We may not realise that there are ways of changing the engineering specification to make it a different machine.

The same applies to other specialists—accounts, distribution, research, to name but a few—who could bring their expertise to bear on the discussion and help lead towards a breaking out of the deadlock.

6. Give a minor concession

Giving a minor concession can help break a deadlock. There's often something worth little to you that is valued by the other side. It's almost worth keeping something back just in case you get into a deadlock.

The stationery supplier offers me a free clock or pen if I place an order *now.* The item costs him pence, but it may be worth several pounds to me.

A word of warning, though: If I don't want the clock or pen, there's no point in him telling me how much it's worth or how much

I've saved. It's in a sense not a concession to me. After all, I never wanted it in the first place.

7. Speak off the record

Another way of dealing with a deadlock is to take the other person to the bar for a drink and say: 'Look, I couldn't possibly say this officially, but . . .' By making a comment off the record and getting an off-the-record response you may well be able to see each other's position clearer than in the more formal negotiating setting.

Many things have been sorted out over a beer, a meal or a game of golf. The informal setting can help to break the deadlock.

Beware of reaching agreements through the haze of alcohol. Some people use alcohol as a tactic for getting you to agree to something. They may appear to be the worse for wear because of drink, but come the morning—when they remind you how much you gave away last night—you'll realise that they were actually as sober as a judge all the time!

Many things have been sorted out over a beer, a meal or a game of golf. The informal setting can help to break the deadlock

8. Tell a funny or relevant story

One of the best ways of relieving the tension of a deadlock is to tell a story. The story could be about how a deadlock was sorted out in another situation. Or it could be a funny story. This is a form of the pacing and leading we talked about in chapter 4: 'Building Rapport'.

The key with using a story to relieve the tension is the 'pattern interrupt'. *If you always do what you've always done, you'll always get what you've always got.* As an excellent negotiator you will want to change the pattern regularly.

If you are caught in the trap of monotony, it's time to do something different. Doing something different changes people's mental state and allows you to start afresh. In a sense, what you do is irrelevant. You could lie on the floor, kicking, screaming and biting the carpet. It might be more socially acceptable, though, to tell a story.

In a particularly stressful situation, people's sense of humour goes down the tube. They get frustrated, irritated and annoyed. Telling a funny story that has nothing to do with what you are talking about helps to break the pattern and enables people to think clearly again.

I heard a true story about a robber who went into a building society and passed a note over the counter demanding £5000 in used £5 notes.

We only have £10 notes, the cashier wrote on the piece of paper and passed it back to him.

The robber read the message and couldn't cope with the change of plan. Looking shocked, he turned, marched out of the building and disappeared into the crowded High Street.

The pattern has been broken. Almost without knowing it, the cashier had used a brilliant 'pattern interrupt'.

One of my favourite stories that I've told on many occasions to break a deadlock is about a time I heard when a British trainer was leading a business course in New York. It was in the days when everyone was expected to go jogging first thing in the morning.

The trainer was out jogging through Central Park one morning when another man bumped into him. Ever fearful of being mugged, he immediately checked his back pocket. Lo and behold, his wallet wasn't there!

Quickly, the trainer raced after the man. Anger was welling up from within him. Being an American, the runner didn't know what a rugby tackle was—until the trainer grabbed him from behind and threw him to the ground.

'Give me the wallet!' the trainer demanded loudly.

Meekly, he handed it over and the trainer stuck it in his pocket. Then he jumped up, turned on his tracks and raced back to the hotel, terrified that the same thing would happen again. Eventually, he got back to the safety of his hotel room and collapsed on the bed.

NEGOTIATING NUGGET:

Excellent negotiators set their targets higher and higher; average negotiators find ways to play it safe.

Gasping to get his breath back he turned his head to one side.

There on the bedside table was his wallet!

Summary

Deadlines—several kinds:
❏ Fixed deadlines
❏ Deadlines on the move
❏ Flexible deadlines
❏ Negotiated deadlines
Deadlines are best fixed and understood by both parties.

Deadlocks—ways of breaking out:
❏ Limit your power
❏ Make a hot-line call
❏ Change the time or money
❏ Change the negotiator or team
❏ Bring in the specialist
❏ Give a minor concession
❏ Speak off the record
❏ Tell a funny or relevant story

11
Get on the Blower and Blow It

Negotiating on the phone is like trying to swim in jelly. Even though you might get there in the end, it's a lot of hard work for very little reward.

Occasionally, using the phone has its advantages for the negotiator. For instance, it has the element of surprise. Usually, though, the negatives far outweigh the positives. More negotiations lead to a win-lose outcome on the phone than when the two parties talk face to face. If you get on the blower to do a deal you may end up blowing the outcome.

On those rare occasions when you must negotiate on the phone, make sure you are well prepared with plenty of facts and information at your fingertips. Mistakes are easy to make—and they can be very costly.

Negative factors

Be aware of the following negative factors in phone negotiations:

1. *By juggling too many balls simultaneously you're likely to drop one*—see the rest of the list.

2. Most phones *fail to show the other negotiator's facial expressions.*

3. It is *difficult to check facts and figures* or to make a presentation without a fax machine.

4. It is *not as easy to stop interruptions* as when you are face to face.

5. It's *hard to concentrate* when we can't see the other person.

6. Phone calls usually *come just at the wrong moment*—when you've got other things on your mind.

NEGOTIATING NUGGET:

The skill in negotiating on the telephone is to avoid it like the plague.

NOTES

7. *Basic calculations become difficult with the pressure of time.*

8. It's *easy to forget important aspects* of the deal.

9. *The caller has the advantage of surprise,* and this works against you if someone is calling you.

10. If you are *caught off guard* by the phone you may not have your diary, calculator or information at your fingertips.

NEGOTIATING NUGGET:

Get the other person to make concessions first. Keep yours ready as spare ammunition.

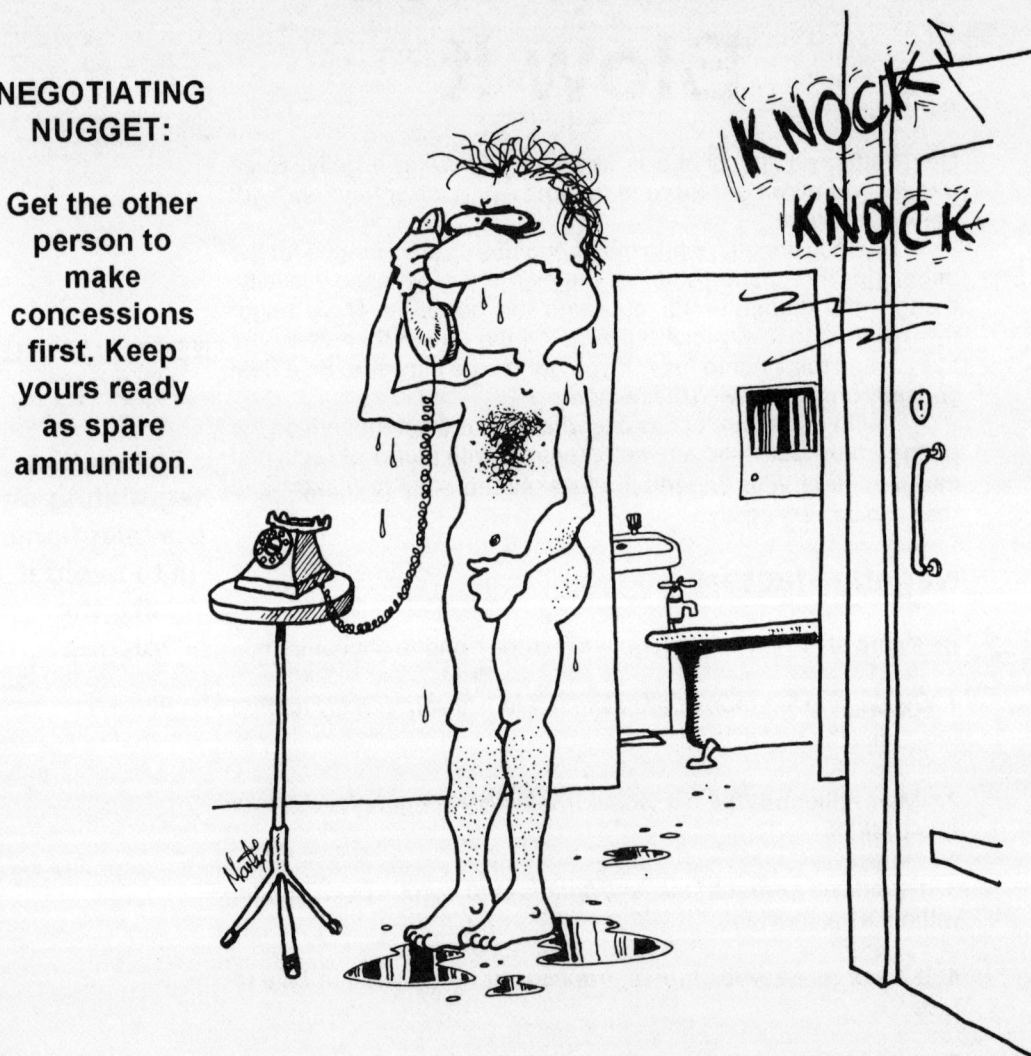

Phone calls usually come just at the wrong moment—when you've got other things on your mind

11. There is *pressure to make a decision quickly*.

12. It's *easier to misunderstand the other party* than when you meet across a table.

13. There is *less time to think*—silence implies to the other person that you've stopped listening.

14. Other people find it *easier to say no* if they can't see you.

One way to avoid phone negotiations is to use a secretary —or your voice mail—as a buffer. If you happen to answer the phone, say you're busy. Then phone back at a time when you will have the initiative.

Positive factors

The phone is great for contacting people who are otherwise hard to talk with. Psychologists have concluded that people can't resist a ringing phone. Once they've picked up the phone they find it hard to put it down again.

Quick deals are usually bad for one party or the other, and phone negotiations are the ultimate quick deals. Yet occasionally a phone call is better than meeting someone in person. For instance, you can:

1. *Talk without listening*

2. *Reduce travel costs*

3. *Act tough*

4. *Say no with ease*

5. *Seem determined*

6. *Prevent discussion*

7. *Interrupt regularly*

8. *Limit the amount of information* you give

9. *Be on the same level* as the other person

10. *Appear relaxed* about a difficult situation

NEGOTIATING NUGGET:

Use the telephone to talk with people who avoid you.

Tips for phone negotiations

On the rare occasions when you decide to use the phone to negotiate, make sure you are well prepared before you enter into negotiation. I suggest you take on board the following ideas:

1. *Rehearse* what you're going to say.

2. Have a *written list of points to tick off* as you cover them in the negotiation.

3. Make sure you have your *background information* as well as a *diary, pen, paper and calculator* on hand before you make the call.

4. Take notes as you talk, *confirm the conversation in writing* and keep your original notes.

5. When other people call you, listen carefully and *negotiate a time when you can call them back.*

6. Make sure you *get all the relevant facts* from the other party.

7. *Talk less so that the other person talks more.*

8. *Call the person back if the deal you've agreed is unclear* or the figures don't add up when you put the phone down.

9. *Avoid giving an immediate response;* tell the other person you'll phone back later.

10. *If you want to avoid a 'no' answer, steer clear of the phone.*

11. *Stand up when you talk.* This will help you feel more in control.

Summary

Negative factors in phone negotiations:
☐ Calls cost money
☐ Phones don't show facial expressions
☐ Difficult to check facts and figures
☐ Difficult to stop interruptions
☐ Difficult to concentrate
☐ Calls come at the wrong moment
☐ Basic calculations become difficult
☐ Easy to forget important aspects
☐ Caller has the advantage of surprise
☐ You may not have your diary, calculator or information
☐ Pressure to make a decision quickly
☐ Easy to misunderstand
☐ Less time to think
☐ Easier for the other person to say no

Positive factors in phone negotiations:
☐ Talk without listening
☐ Reduce travel costs
☐ Act tough
☐ Say no with ease
☐ Seem determined
☐ Prevent discussion
☐ Interrupt regularly
☐ Limit information
☐ Be on the same level
☐ Appear relaxed

Tips for phone negotiations:
☐ Rehearse
☐ List points to cover
☐ Get information, diary, pen, paper and calculator
☐ Take notes, confirm in writing
☐ Negotiate a time to call back
☐ Get relevant facts
☐ Talk less than the other person
☐ Call back with queries
☐ Avoid an immediate response
☐ Don't phone if you want to avoid a 'no' answer
☐ Stand up when you talk

NEGOTIATING NUGGET:

A good negotiator makes the other party work to get a concession. People don't appreciate something for nothing.

12
There's No Such Thing as a Free Lunch

A good way to break out of a deadlock is to retreat to a more informal setting. In the relaxed atmosphere of a restaurant or a pub you may well be able to find ways around the deadlock. Of course, someone will have to pay for it in one way or another. In order to ensure a level playing field the simple advice is: Pay for your own. After all, there's no such thing as a free lunch.

In another context you may be taken out for a meal as part of the negotiating process. Usually the seller pays and the buyer is treated. When the food is great and the wine is flowing, you may find yourself giving away a concession that you will later regret. The relationship between buyer and seller will, over time, always fall in favour of the seller. So be aware before you accept the free lunch.

It may be worth every negotiator carrying their own breathalyser—if you're over the limit for driving, you're certainly not fit to negotiate!

The next time you as the seller decide to offer concessions of any sort—even a free lunch—remember that they can work against you. Give something away for nothing and it won't be appreciated or will be viewed with suspicion. Make the other person work to gain every centimetre in the negotiation and you'll have a satisfied customer.

NEGOTIATING NUGGET:

Concessions will be valued more if they aren't won easily.

Concessions? No chance!

You've been instructed by your senior manager that under no circumstances are you to give any concessions. At the same time you are asked to help the buyer feel satisfied with the deal. How can these two be reconciled? It seems impossible.

The answer is by making concessions that give nothing away. Here are some suggestions:

1. Treat the other people with *respect.* Be *friendly* and *pleasant* in the negotiations.

It may be worth every negotiator carrying their own breathalyser—if you're over the limit for driving, you're certainly not fit to negotiate!

NEGOTIATING NUGGET:

Avoid giving concessions too soon. The thirstier a person is, the better the water tastes.

2. Use your active listening skills to *understand* what's being said (see chapter 5: 'Listening and Questioning Skills').

3. *Explain* your position clearly and thoroughly.

4. *Encourage* the other people to check out the facts.

5. Be ready to *go over the same ground* again and again, even if you are at risk of sounding like a broken record.

6. *Back up what you say* with evidence.

7. Point out that other competent, well respected people are being *treated in exactly the same way.*

8. If possible, make *promises about future concessions;* explain how the deal will give the future satisfaction you've promised.

9. *Give the other people information* about the product or marketplace.

10. Get people higher up in your organisation to *commit themselves to ensuring the buyer's satisfaction.*

Chain reaction

Walk down the average high street and you'll see dozens of signs declaring boldly: Massive Price Reductions, Final Sale, Sale Must End Saturday, Closing Down Sale, Reduced This Week Only.

Walk down the same high street in six months' time and you are likely to see a similar number of special offer signs. Why? Shoppers have come to expect concessions every time they buy clothes, shoes and household goods. Concessions breed concessions. They can also reflect a recession.

The next time you as a seller are tempted to offer a concession, put yourself in the buyer's shoes. How will the seller take it? If you give a large concession this time, the buyer may ask for even more next time. Is that what you really want?

Ask yourself: What will the seller make of this concession? What will he want from me in future negotiations?

Offering a concession can be a kindness. A concession that goes too far is a case of 'killing with kindness'—and you might be the one who ends up dead on the floor.

Concessions that work

Over the years I've learned by experience that concessions can be either a blessing or a curse in negotiations. The excellent negotiator strives to make them a blessing so that there is a win-win outcome for both parties. I think of them in terms of familiar sayings:

1. 'Marry in haste, repent at leisure'

Being too hasty with offering a concession sets you up for problems in the future. 'You gave me that concession last time—I expect you to do the same this time.' Be like the tortoise: 'More haste, less speed.' Offer your concessions only when you are well into the negotiation.

2. 'Line upon line, line upon line, here a little, there a little'

When you give concessions little and often, both parties are far more likely to be happy with the outcome than if you dish out a major one. Passing a box of chocolates around six times is far more impressive than passing it around once and asking everyone to choose six chocolates.

NEGOTIATING NUGGET:

Exchange is no robbery. Make sure you get something for every concession you give.

3. 'Look before you leap'

Negotiators who do badly often make their first concession on something fundamentally important to the deal. Successful negotiators look before they jump in with both feet.

4. 'Time waits for no man'

A time limit is good for everyone to concentrate their thoughts. Skilled negotiators work towards a clear deadline.

Make your
starting price
high as a
seller or low
as a buyer.
Have a reason
why you start
there.

5. 'Look after the pennies and the pounds will take care of themselves'

Low offers at the start often improve a buyer's results. Don't bury your Talents; be like the Wise Steward and use them to make even greater profits.

6. 'One swallow doesn't make a summer'

One large concession often results in a poor negotiation. Keep them small and you'll both be happy.

7. 'It's not the joke—it's the way you tell it'

As the comedian knows the exact moment to tell a particular joke, so the negotiator knows the right time to bring in a concession. With the right punchline the comedian gets a laugh and the negotiator gets the deal.

Finally, remember that as with other aspects of negotiation, concessions don't automatically guarantee that a deal is struck.

'Don't count your chickens before they're hatched!'

Summary

Concessions that give nothing away:

- ☐ Be friendly and pleasant; treat people with respect
- ☐ Listen with understanding
- ☐ Explain
- ☐ Encourage
- ☐ Go over the same ground again and again
- ☐ Give evidence
- ☐ Treat others in the same way
- ☐ Make promises about future concessions
- ☐ Give information
- ☐ Get others in your organisation to ensure buyer's satisfaction

NEGOTIATING NUGGET:

If you say: 'I'll think about that,' you've already made a concession.

Concessions breed concessions. Think of the golden rules as well known sayings:

- ☐ 'Marry in haste, repent at leisure'
- ☐ 'Line upon line, line upon line, here a little, there a little'
- ☐ 'Look before you leap'
- ☐ 'Time waits for no man'
- ☐ 'Look after the pennies and the pounds will take care of themselves'
- ☐ 'One swallow doesn't make a summer'
- ☐ 'It's not the joke—it's the way you tell it'
- ☐ 'Don't count your chickens before they're hatched!'

13
The Power Balance

What is power? It is the ability of one party to persuade and influence another party towards their point of view. In a perfect world you and I would have the same amount of power. In practice, one of us often has more power than the other.

Power is a flow of influence between two people. In itself, it is neither good nor bad. Power is simply power. When used wrongly, power can have a damaging effect. When used for good, it is one of the greatest forces known to humanity.

In negotiation it's important to recognise power and to assess the power of each side. Much of this has to do with personal perception—the way we each see our own and other people's power. This is directly related to our own personal self-esteem and the feeling of pride we have because we are part of a particular organisation.

If I have high self-esteem about myself, as well as my organisation and its products, I'll be better able to handle the negotiation than if I have low self-esteem. If I have low self-esteem, I become apathetic, almost giving away my power to the other party.

Once you understand the power issues on both sides you will be better able to take the steps in the planning stage (see chapter 6: 'The Seven Steps to Negotiation').

**NEGOTIATING NUGGET:
Learn to say no without smiling. People will then believe that you have no more concessions up your sleeve.**

Automatic response

One of the interesting things about power—which includes influencing and persuasion—is the way we respond almost automatically in certain situations. It's almost as if we have a preprogrammed response to certain sorts of power.

For instance, if a policeman stands out in front of your car and puts up his hand, you probably hit the brakes without even realising it. The authority invested in him has automatically affected your response.

Similarly, the whole Roman Catholic church bows to the power of the Pope and seeks to follow his dictates on marriage, birth control and abortion. From my point of view, as a non-Catholic, I find it difficult to grasp that an unmarried man who has never had children could pass dictates on the subject. Yet, because of his position, he has the power and people tend to follow what he says.

There's no right or wrong; it's just a fact that Catholics accept this particular value system.

Power imbalance

What happens if there's a power imbalance? Supposing there's a sales manager who's a really expert negotiator going in with a rookie purchaser. Would the sales manager take advantage of the situation?

Research has shown that the sales manager who is an excellent negotiator makes sure the inexperienced buyer doesn't get his fingers badly burned. He ensures that the buyer gets a good deal because he knows that buyer will then return one day. He is after building long-term relationships, not making short-term gains.

If the inexperienced purchaser doesn't have the power, he may need to escalate things. Trouble could be ahead if he uses escalation as a tactic.

Types of power

There are many kinds of power. I want to highlight seven:

1. The power of liking

a. Looks

It's a sad reflection on society that people who are deemed to be better looking than others will have more to influence on others than people who aren't so good looking. Looks can include facial features, height, weight, muscles and dress sense. There are also non-visual aspects such as friendliness, courtesy, understanding and listening ability.

Tests have shown that people in negotiation are more easily persuaded and influenced by people who are attractive than by those who don't match up to society's unwritten standards. For the excellent negotiator, it's important in this not to take people at face value. However, the fact remains that this is a major factor in many people's minds.

b. 'Like us'

It's a well known fact that people who are like us, like us. If the other negotiator likes you, this gives you added power. People who have similar opinions to us are more easily influenced than others who are very different. The same applies to people who have similar traits and who speak like us.

c. Dress sense and hobbies/interests

Think about what you wear to a meeting. If you dress in a way similar to the other party you are more likely to be acceptable. What hobbies and interests do you have that are common to you both? By taking these factors into account you will push the power of persuasion in your favour. The other side are then more likely to be influenced by your arguments.

d. Conditioning

People are constantly being conditioned when they meet you. The other person gets to know you and is more easily swayed by your suggestions.

e. Who you know

The people you know and the ones who you have worked with are also factors in the process of developing your liking levels.

f. Matching and mirroring

People like those who reflect back to them the way they talk and their mannerisms. Matching and mirroring is crucial in developing the power of liking (see chapter 4: 'Building Rapport').

It's important that all this is done with integrity. If you use the liking factors to manipulate people, abusing your power, you will only ever abuse that power once. What we are talking here is a genuine interest in the other people and of finding ways to come to an agreement.

2. The power of 'one favour deserves another'

In negotiation I always try to get the other person to give a concession first. There is something within our makeup, however, that makes us want to return one favour with another. If the other person gives something to me, I want to give something in return. It's almost an obligation. 'Let me give you something' in most people triggers off the need to respond.

This can be a very powerful process. If I offer the other party something, they may well want to return like for like.

Remember, though, that if someone is offering you a concession in good faith, there's no need to feel obliged to give something in return. Resist the urge. If people are using this natural urge as leverage on you and you don't respond, they may get quite irritated with you. If that's happening, don't get into a tit for tat agreement.

Bear in mind the rule of thumb for concession giving is that you give 40 and the other side give you 60 in return. (For more

NEGOTIATING NUGGET:

Concession exchanges needn't be evenly matched. The other side might be satisfied with the pretty little marbles you give them just as much as you are with the big marbles they give you.

on concessions see chapter 12: 'There's No Such Thing as a Free Lunch'.)

3. The power of authority

There are three forms of power in authority:

a. Position

This is the notion that someone is more senior to another person so you give due deference to that person.

I've known people in negotiations who make sure that their job title matches up with that of the other person so the balance of power is equal.

Someone I knew was an ordinary Sales Executive yet was selling a particular product around Europe. He called himself the European Sales Manager of that particular product—which is what he was—and as a result he was treated in the European companies as someone very senior. By changing the label to match that of the people he was negotiating with he did extremely well, even though he was still just an ordinary Sales Executive in the UK.

b. Legitimacy

Because people are in a certain position of power, they must be right. Legitimate power has a hypnotic effect on people. Putting a price tag on something brings an element of legitimacy. Because it's the price that is presented, it becomes legitimate power. Very few people ever argue with that.

c. Knowledge and expertise

There is no doubt that knowledge is power. People who are experts on a particular subject wield an enormous amount of power. They know more about the product, market or organisation than anyone else. It pays to have an expert on hand or to ensure that you yourself become that expert on the product, market and company because that will increase your power.

4. The power of commitment and consistency

Commitment, loyalty and friendship are the three foundation stones of power.

People who are committed to the success of negotiation have the strength needed to go the extra mile. They will find ways of reaching the goal whatever gets in the way. 'I'll walk a million miles for one of your smiles' is their attitude towards negotiation.

Those who believe in their organisation and its viewpoint stand much firmer, and people will respect them for that. People loyal to their company will gain more power than people with a wealth of knowledge and little commitment.

There is also power in consistency. People who are consistent in their beliefs, behaviours and attitudes are well respected. Most people prefer to work with someone who is consistent. When I deal with you as a consistent person I know that what you *say* you'll do you will in fact do. I know that your attitude, beliefs and values are all consistent. You present as WYSIWYG—What You See Is What You Get. I know exactly where I am with you.

Of course, if I am being consistent with unscrupulous negotiators, they could take advantage of this by manipulating me. Nevertheless, the best negotiators are committed and consistent.

Once I've made a decision, I'll support that decision come hell or high water. I'll find reasons for being consistent. This can work for bad as well as for good. If my consistency is blinkered, I can get myself caught in a blind alley. I'll constantly find reasons why I've made that decision. I could be cornered and end up agreeing to things I wouldn't normally have agreed to.

There's an old trick used by negotiators in estate agents. Imagine you're very interested in buying a particular house.

'What sort of furniture have you got?' the estate agent asks.

You tell him and he asks: 'How do you think your furniture will fit into this house?'

NEGOTIATING NUGGET:

It's OK to back down from a concession. Until you sign on the dotted line everything's in the melting-pot.

Once you're committed to buying the house you do everything you can to reinforce that commitment

Suddenly, in your mind you've started moving in. You think about where each piece of furniture goes. If a piece doesn't quite fit, you start planning how to make it fit. Then you think about one piece of furniture that you can't fit in. 'We can keep that in the garage,' you say.

Once you're committed to buying the house you do everything you can to reinforce that commitment. Buying a house is often done on a subjective basis—'I just feel this is the right house.' Then you start finding reasons to move in.

It's fulfilling to negotiate with people who are really committed to success, to their organisation and to their products. I like them to be consistent in the way they behave towards me, in their attitudes and the beliefs they have. I know where I am with those sort of people.

NEGOTIATING
NUGGET:

There is
always a limit
to power. No
one side in a
negotiation
ever has total
power.

The down side is that if I'm committed and consistent I may be trapped into doing something that I don't particularly want to do. Commitment and consistency can then lead to compromise. I've talked myself into buying something.

I once bought a car that was really too expensive for me. The car salesman asked me: 'Are you sure you can afford this?' I was caught by my own commitment, consistency—and ego. I bought the car.

5. The power of no power

The power of no power is based on the fact that organisations are busy and under the pressure of restraint. It is very useful under such circumstances to say: 'Sorry, I don't have the power to decide that.' It is entirely up to you to decide who you will give that power to. It could even be to the cleaning staff, if you so choose.

For the negotiators on the other side, this sticking point can be very irritating. It is difficult to negotiate with someone who says: 'It's more than my job's worth to agree to that.'

The 'job's worths' of this world can drive the negotiator crazy. When they speak up, that's the end of the negotiation because they have no power. On the other hand, the power of limited power can be a useful tool to have in your toolkit when things reach a difficult point or when you need time to think.

When I negotiate for training I sort out all the details of what the course is going to contain. When the other person wants to talk about money I'll say: 'Sorry, I don't have the power to deal with that. You'll have to talk to someone in my marketing department.' It's not that I can't discuss money. It's just that when I've got my hat on as the trainer I don't get involved in the money. What I'm after is getting the best training course together.

6. The power of scarcity

There are two forms of scarcity:

a. Rarity

It is a fact that antiques are worth more because there aren't many of them around. They are rare or unique, and therefore have intrinsic value.

b. Shortage

Antiques also go up in value because one person wants a particular item and others see that and want that same item as well. If there is a rumour of a sugar shortage, for instance, suddenly everyone buys up vast quantities of sugar 'just in case'. In hot summers when wasps are on the rampage, wasp-sting products become a rare commodity and shops will pay over the odds to get them.

In negotiation, if you happen to have the sort of goods and services that fill either of these two sorts of scarcity—rarity or shortage—that puts you in a powerful position. Bear in mind that the power is purely perceptual. All you need is for someone to start a rumour that there is a sugar shortage and people buy it like there's no tomorrow.

If I'm offering a service that's the first of its kind in the market place, its success will breed success. The more I'm booked up as a trainer, the more people want me to do training for them. 'If you want a job doing, give it to a busy person.' It works the same the other way round. If you have nothing to do, no-one wants your skills.

The fact that I'm busy and my time is scarce puts me in a powerful position. I have a scarce resource. I can therefore negotiate from a position of power.

If I have lots of time on my hands and reduce my price to get some business, the power shifts to the other side. This sets a precedent of low prices for future negotiations. The other side has the balance of power and this becomes part of the long-term relationship between us.

Another form of scarcity is scarcity of information. This is a very powerful form of persuasion and influence; people will give anything for that information. You want to know more and I'm the only person who can help you.

It doesn't help to give everything away. Information is a useful thing for concession giving. It must never be withheld as a tactic merely to get your own way. See it instead as a valuable scarce commodity that helps you to reach a better deal for all parties concerned.

7. The power of influence

I'm absolutely staggered by the number of Mercedes that have turned up in our road since I bought mine. If someone builds a house extension, there is soon a plague of extensions in the

NEGOTIATING NUGGET:

If you refuse to accept the power I have, my power is worthless.

neighbourhood. Keeping up with the Joneses is a fact of life for most of us, whether we like it or not.

In negotiation many people say: 'I'll do or agree to this as long as I can see other people doing or agreeing to the same.' The social scientists have experimented in this area. They've discovered that people will go to great lengths to do things because those things were what they thought were the society's norms.

It is useful to go into negotiation armed with social proof that other people have used the particular product or service you are offering. If I'm told that other training organisations are finding a particular photocopier beneficial then I will be more ready to consider the same copier. I want to keep up with the other companies. The fact that it does good photocopying is important but not as important as being seen in the same league as other training organisations.

Social proof isn't always a good thing. The other day I was almost triggered into mowing my lawn simply because other people up and down our road were doing it. Yet I knew the ground was wet and the lawn would look worse than when I started. Be aware that just because someone else is using a product or service doesn't necessarily mean it's a good one.

NEGOTIATING NUGGET:

The balance of power in negotiation is in direct proportion to the scarcity of the commodity under negotiation.

Increase your power

Most people have more power than they realise. People who are secure in their own power can take risks—which is a form of power in itself. Those who work hard at a deal gain power; those who are lazy forfeit their right to this form of power. Companies with a lot of business have more power than companies with empty order books.

Above all, power is a matter of attitude. Once people realise the power—or the perceived power—they have, they can explore new ways to find a win-win outcome for all the parties concerned.

It pays to increase your influencing and persuasion power.

Summary

Types of power:

☐ **The power of liking**
      —Looks
      —'Like us'
      —Dress sense and hobbies/interests
      —Conditioning
      —Who you know
      —Matching and mirroring
☐ **The power of 'one favour deserves another'**
☐ **The power of authority**
      —Position
      —Legitimacy
      —Knowledge and expertise
☐ **The power of commitment and consistency**
☐ **The power of no power**
☐ **The power of scarcity**
      —Rarity
      —Shortage
☐ **The power of influence**

How much power you have depends on other people's perception of you.

NEGOTIATING NUGGET:

Power is a fact of life in negotiating. It is neither a good thing nor a bad thing.

14
Up Your Aspirations

Research has shown that people get what they expect. If you reach for the sky you'll soon be flying. If you aim low you'll end up crash-landing.

If you want to be an excellent negotiator, aim your sights high and you will achieve a win-win outcome for both parties. If you aim low you are more likely to end up with a lose-win or lose-lose outcome.

Research has shown that people with high aspirations achieve better results in negotiation than people with low aspirations. Yet both feel satisfied with the result. The man earning £28,000 a year usually wants a job that pays slightly more. So does the man earning £70,000. Each has a level of aspiration directly related to his past performance. The man earning £28,000 cannot conceive of reaching earnings of £70,000. Yet he may have the same qualifications and experience as the man earning £70,000.

The difference between the two is that the man earning the larger amount has a fairly high aspiration while the man on a low income keeps his aspiration levels low.

The poet John Masefield once wrote critically about those with low aspirations: 'Success is the brand on the brow of the man who aimed too low.'

Negotiating Nugget:

If you always do what you've always done, you'll always get what you always got.

Aiming high

Everyone has goals and aspirations. Unless you were rehoused compulsorily, the last house you moved into was itself making a statement about your status goals. Certainly we choose cars more on the status attached to them than on their performance. Are your aspirations based on an unreliable rust heap or a gleaming car that starts first time, every time?

The same attitude applies to the workplace. Do you put up with working for a shoddy, incompetent organisation, or are you able to say that your company is among the best of its kind? Does your company have a healthy corporate self-image aiming for high profit margins? Or is it content to drift along, at best breaking even? Are the staff you work with mediocre or high achievers?

Excellent negotiators aim high and achieve their targets. They trade wishful thinking for firm intentions. So determined are they to reach their goals that they allow no room for falling short of those goals. If they then miss the mark they make adjustments and try again. Failure isn't a word in their vocabulary.

NEGOTIATING NUGGET:

Make a mental note of concessions made on both sides. Be the one to put everything in writing.

Excellent negotiators aim high and achieve their targets

Four stages

Generations of athletes said that the four-minute mile could never be broken. Then, on 6 May 1954, a young medical student with high aspirations and an understanding of the human body went through the pain barrier at Oxford University to cover the distance in an amazing 3 min 59.4 sec.

Roger Bannister raised the aspirations of sports people around the world. The impossible could now be achieved. Other mile-runners, not content merely to break that magical time, raised their aspiration levels higher and higher. As a result, within 40 years of Bannister's achievement, a phenomenal 15 seconds had been knocked off the mile distance.

There are thus four stages to aspiration:

1. Set the standard—the four-minute mile

2. Establish the aspiration level—the four-minute barrier can be broken

3. Raise the aspiration level—progressively knock fractions of a second off the time

4. Celebrate the successes at each stage—enjoy reaching your target times

Satisfaction levels

Our aspiration levels tend to rise when we succeed and go down when we don't. It's important, therefore, to raise our aspiration levels gradually. Massive underachievement can leave any negotiator feeling deflated.

Remember, too, that success is relative. I feel a sense of victory if I can be out of bed by ten o'clock on a Saturday. The milkman can only be content if he has virtually finished a full day's work by then. Psychologist Alfred Adler said: 'What an individual feels as success is unique with him.'

If you come to know that the negotiators on the other team have low aspiration levels, your small concession will be seen by them as a major success. The result will be that both sides feel good about the outcome of the deal.

High achievers

People who set themselves high aspirations tend to work harder, do a better job and value accomplishment more than reward. They measure their success in terms of reaching the goal rather than making a fast buck.

One researcher discovered that people set their aspiration level by balancing the pleasure of success against the displeasure of failure. People who are successful have high aspirations. They aren't ones to gamble; they enjoy winning through their own skill. Success breeds success. People who fear failure avoid the challenges of life. They have low aspiration levels to match their low self-esteem.

This isn't to say that successful negotiators are always persistent. If the goal is too easy they quickly lose interest. On the other hand, they rise to the unexpected challenge by seeking to conquer it.

People who are high achievers take a long-term view of life. They learn how to solve problems, remove objects in the way and through sheer determination achieve the result they are after. They create their own success.

Realistic goals

To exist in today's society you need to have realistic goals in life. If you set goals that are consistent with your own ability and the pressures of the world around you, you'll have healthy aspirations.

If your personal expectations are unrealistic, you are likely to end up frustrated, discouraged and stressed out.

If you have a poor sense of self-worth your aspiration levels will tend to be unbalanced and unrealistic—or just plain low. Aspiration levels are closely linked to a person's self-esteem. If you think well of yourself and have a clear sense of self-identity, you are likely to be a healthy, well-balanced individual. If you haven't got high self-esteem, it's time to change your attitude now.

NEGOTIATING NUGGET:

Set high goals and you will become a high achiever.

Excellent negotiators expect success and set their aspirations high. They are realistic, keep at the task and listen to advice from others.

The boss who tells the negotiator: 'Do the best you can,' is not helping him or her to achieve the best results. Instead ask: 'What's your aspiration level—and how can you raise it even higher?'

Successful negotiators raise their aspiration levels time and time again. As they succeed yet again they are motivated to even greater success. And they celebrate their achievement with a declaration of intent to themselves: 'Up your aspirations!'

Summary

Everyone has goals and aspirations. Excellent negotiators aim high and achieve their targets. There are four stages to aspiration:

☐ Set the standard
☐ Establish the aspiration level
☐ Raise the aspiration level
☐ Celebrate the successes at each stage

People who set themselves high aspirations:

☐ Work harder
☐ Do a better job
☐ Value accomplishment more than reward
☐ Take a long-term view of life
☐ Learn how to solve problems
☐ Achieve the result they are after
☐ Create their own success
☐ Have a clear sense of self-identity
☐ Expect success
☐ Keep at the task
☐ Listen to advice from others

Wallchart
Summary

The following two pages contain a summary of the summaries in this book. Use them to remind youself of the salient points in being an excellent negotiator.

You have permission to make up to four photocopies of the two pages for your personal use providing you include on the photocopies the copyright details. My advice is that you enlarge each page on your photocopier to A3 size.

Pin them up where you can see them. Then remind yourself daily about the negotiating skills you have learned. And remember, the goal is to work towards a win-win outcome for all the parties concerned.

Up Your Aspirations:

How to Succeed Every Time

1. Become a team player
2. Cultivate support
3. Plan to plan
4. Develop sound business judgment
5. Grow in handling ambiguity and conflict
6. Set higher targets
7. Learn to listen
8. Get involved
9. Seek mutual satisfaction
10. Have an enquiring mind
11. Come to understand people
12. Become confident
13. Be willing to bring in experts
14. Have a sense of humour
15. Be happy with yourself

What Makes People Tick?

The fundamental rules of communication are:
- ❐ Respect the other person's model of the world
- ❐ Remember that they do things for their reasons, not yours
- ❐ Communication is the response you get
- ❐ Feedback is the secret of future success
- ❐ The negotiator with the most flexibility has the most effect

Communication model:
- ❐ We take in information through our **senses**—what we see, hear, feel, smell and taste.
- ❐ We then reduce that information down by filtering through our life's experiences: **delete, distort** and **generalise.**
- ❐ At any one time we can only deal with **five to nine piece of information** at a conscious level.
- ❐ We pass the information through our **filters**: language, mem-ories, decisions, perceptions, values, beliefs and attitudes.
- ❐ That creates an **internal representation** of the event—the pictures in your head and the way you might talk to yourself.
- ❐ In turn that affects your **state**—how you feel about it. If you have a good picture you feel great; if you have a bad picture you feel lousy.
- ❐ Those two affect your **physiology**—thinking, feeling, stance.
- ❐ Your internal representation, state and physiology have a direct bearing on your **behaviour.**
- ❐ Your behaviour becomes the **input** into the other person. If your input is in a positive way that matches the other person's model of the world then we have good communication.

Building Rapport

The process can be speeded up by *matching and mirroring.*

1. **Physiology**
   a. Gestures
   b. Posture
   c. Breathing
   d. Facial expressions
2. **Voice**
   a. Tone
   b. Clarity
   c. Speed
   d. Volume
3. **Words**
   a. Key words
   b. Common experience
   c. Predicates—sight, sound, touch and nonspecific sensing
   d. Global/specific filters
   Once rapport is built, the negotiator is in position to *pace and lead.*

The Top Ten Tactics

1. **Good Guy, Bad Guy**—avoid getting sucked in
2. **Taking It Higher**—challenge it on the spot
3. **The Nibble**—demand two concessions for every one given
4. **Red Herring**—set it on one side
5. **Put It in Writing**—if there's a price in writing, it's usually negotiable.
6. **What If?**—think through possibilities from the buyer's point of view
7. **A Bridge Too Far**—be tough with the other person and hold your ground
8. **Funny Money**—counter them head on
9. **You Must Be Joking!**—one of the most effective counter measures is silence
10. **Eating an Elephant**—agree ever-diminishing discounts

The Helping Handful

1. Competition
2. Co-operation
3. Organisation
4. Attitude
5. Personal factors

Up Your Aspirations

- ❐ Set the standard
- ❐ Establish the aspiration level
- ❐ Raise the aspiration level
- ❐ Celebrate the successes at each stage

People who set themselves high aspirations:
- ❐ Work harder
- ❐ Do a better job
- ❐ Value accomplishment more than reward
- ❐ Take a long-term view of life
- ❐ Learn how to solve problems
- ❐ Achieve the result they are after
- ❐ Create their own success
- ❐ Have a clear sense of self-identity
- ❐ Expect success
- ❐ Keep at the task
- ❐ Listen to advice from others

Listening and Questioning Skills

Listening involves:
- ❐ Mirroring—repeating back what the other person has just said
- ❐ Undivided attention—keeping your mind focused on the conversation
- ❐ Separate messenger from message—directing your feelings appropriately
- ❐ Active listening—smiling, nodding and open body posture
- ❐ Changing from listening to questioning
  - Clarify
  - Check understanding
  - Reflect back
- ❐ Questioning for information
  - Open questions
  - Probing questions
  - Closed question
  - Summarising
- ❐ Questioning to get the whole picture

The Power Balance

Types of power:
- ❐ The power of liking
- ❐ The power of 'one favour deserves another'
- ❐ The power of authority
- ❐ The power of commitment and consistency
- ❐ The power of no power
- ❐ The power of scarcity
- ❐ The power of influence

Negotiating program using NLP

The Seven Steps to Negotiation
1. Define the overall purpose
2. Examine the background
3. Decide the strategy
4. Specify objective
5. Assess the bargaining power of each side
6. Plan arguments
7. Arrange your team and tactics

Breaking Out of Deadlines and Deadlocks
Deadlines—several kinds:
- ☐ Fixed deadlines
- ☐ Deadlines on the move
- ☐ Flexible deadlines
- ☐ Negotiated deadlines

Deadlines are best fixed and understood by both parties.
Deadlocks—ways of breaking out:
- ☐ Limit your power
- ☐ Make a hot-line call
- ☐ Change the time or money
- ☐ Change the negotiator or team
- ☐ Bring in the specialist
- ☐ Give a minor concession
- ☐ Speak off the record
- ☐ Tell a funny or relevant story

There's No Such Thing as a Free Lunch
Concessions that give nothing away:
- ☐ Be friendly and pleasant; treat people with respect
- ☐ Listen with understanding
- ☐ Explain
- ☐ Encourage
- ☐ Go over the same ground again and again
- ☐ Give evidence
- ☐ Treat others in the same way
- ☐ Make promises about future concessions
- ☐ Give information
- ☐ Get others in your organisation to ensure buyer's satisfaction

Concessions breed concessions. Think of the golden rules as well known sayings:
- ☐ 'Marry in haste, repent at leisure'
- ☐ 'Line upon line, line upon line, here a little, there a little'
- ☐ 'Look before you leap'
- ☐ 'Time waits for no man'
- ☐ 'Look after the pennies and the pounds will take care of themselves'
- ☐ 'One swallow doesn't make a summer'
- ☐ 'It's not the joke—it's the way you tell it'
- ☐ 'Don't count your chickens before they're hatched!'

The Seven Stages in the Negotiation Process
What's on offer:
1. Present the ideal outcome
2. Listen carefully for all the information, including hidden signals
   —ask questions
   —give your own hidden signals
3. Amend the proposals as necessary
   —continue asking questions

The core of the process:
4. Packaging—finding new ways of presenting the product or service
5. Bargaining—concession making

Ensuring a successful ending:
6. Closing and making sure agreements are sorted out
7. Contracting to ensure that all parties know and understand precisely what has been agreed

Black Belt Techniques
Get into a positive state
- ☐ Sit up straight
- ☐ Keep your confidence
- ☐ Look the other person straight in the eye
- ☐ Slow your voice down
- ☐ Add more authority to your voice by talking further back in your throat
- ☐ Speak to the other person directly
- ☐ Avoid any weak qualifiers—hopefully, maybe, possibly, per-haps, etc
- ☐ Counter any untrue statements
- ☐ Make sure you get your point over

Ways of handling aggression:
1. Call the other person's bluff
2. Withdraw
3. Divide and conquer
4. Keep things simple
5. Avoid defence
6. Plan your strategy
7. Take time to listen
8. Keep on track

Get on the Blower and Blow It
Tips for phone negotiations:
- ☐ Rehearse
- ☐ List points to cover
- ☐ Get information, diary, pen, paper and calculator
- ☐ Take notes, confirm in writing
- ☐ Negotiate a time to call back
- ☐ Get relevant facts
- ☐ Talk less than the other person
- ☐ Call back with queries
- ☐ Avoid an immediate response
- ☐ Don't phone if you want to avoid a 'no' answer
- ☐ Stand up when you talk

Training, Consultancy & Personal Development

In addition to the Negotiating Program, we offer other training, including:

❏ Business skills
❏ Cultural change
❏ Leadership
❏ Management development
❏ Presentation
❏ Stress
❏ Teamwork
❏ Communication
❏ Trainer training
❏ All levels of NLP training
❏ Individual coaching and mentoring

For further details of running programs within your organisation contact:

Robert Smith
Telephone: 01788-822141
e-mail: robert-smith@freeuk.com

or:

**Robert Smith & Caroline Suggett
ROM Consultancy Ltd
Eastlands Court, St Peter's Road
RUGBY
Warwickshire
CV21 3QP
Tel: 01788 555040   Fax: 01788 555041**

NOTES

NOTES

NOTES

NOTES

NOTES

NOTES

NOTES

NOTES